SOUTH INDIAN CUISINE – THE RESEARCHER'S GUIDE BOOK

DR ANSHUMALI PANDEY

Contents

Foreword

The books written by **Dr Anshumali Pandey** are essentially a banquet arising from an experience of over 25 years of Professional life and have boiled down to crisp and accurate writing on his favourite subjects. Hospitality Sector champion requires to be a specialist in many fields and Dr Pandey is one of them. His knowledge is evident from the spectrum of subjects which he has chosen for his books so far, which ranges from being a specialist chef, to Master of Human resources, to Education and to love for children, and topped with Spirituality.

South Indian Cuisine - The Researcher's Guide Book is a research based collection of information on the subject. This book consists of authentic recipes and information on the classical South Indian Cookery. To know the Cuisine in the correct perspective the knowledge of the local Geography, History, Climate, Culture and festivals are and important asset. The Author has taken care to ensure that all such relatable information is woven in the form of a story so that the new Research scholars of Indian Cookery in general and South Indian Cookery in particular gets benefited.

CHAPTER ONE

Introduction to South Indian Cuisine

Introduction to South Indian Cuisine:

Andhra Pradesh:

Andhra Pradesh is one of the south Indian states and is positioned in the coastal area towards the south eastern part of the country and because of its location in the merging area of the Deccan plateau and the coastal plains and also transverse by Krishna and Godavari rivers, the state experiences varied physical features. This typical topography of the state enables it acquire rich and heterogeneous culture and heritage. Being ruled by some of the famous dynasties in the historical times, this south Indian state is said to have a rich cultural heritage. Historically the state is known as the — Rice Bowl of India. Andhra cuisine or Telugu cuisine is a cuisine of South India native to the Telugu people from the states of Andhra Pradesh and Telangana. Generally known for its tangy, hot and spicy taste, the cooking is very diverse due to the vast spread of the people and varied topological regions.

Tamil Nadu:

Tamil Nadu has always been a hub for food connoisseurs to take a great pleasure of some of the finest traditional cuisine in the country. The state is reckoned to be one of the best places in India for offering a bagful of culinary treasure for tourists to savour. But, the fascinating things about Tamil Nadu are the touch of their customary culture which is served with its every delectable fare. Idli, Sambar, Dosa, Uttapam, and Vada are just a few names whenever it comes to popular South Indian food. Whereas, there are some other equally popular traditional foods of Tamil Nadu that are not much in outside world except the region but are sure to delight your taste buds. The region is known to offer a wide variety of both vegetarian and non – vegetarian dishes with each holding a unique flavor some taste.

Tamil Nadu is also recognized for its varied range of spices which are also exported in different nations like Chillies, Tamarind, Cardamom, Coriander, Pepper, Curry Leaves, Cloves, and Mint. The state also bids an extensive range of tea, coffee, banana and coconut, which together with other fares, makes Tamil Nadu one of the best food getaways in India. Whereas, the food habit remains almost the same in all season as the weather of the state does not fluctuate much. The popular cuisine of Tamil Nadu perfectly connects with its people and is incredibly dipped with the right amount and quantity of spices along with all other ingredients.

Kerala:

Kerala, lovingly called "God"s own country" is truly a land of eternal bliss and a tropical Eden with the mesmerizing beauty of its sun bathed golden seashores edged with abundant coconut trees, the zigzag rocky terrain of the Western Ghats, straggling plantations and paddy fields, the cerulean lagoons and the bountiful rivers and mighty waterfalls, fascinating bio – diversity of its flora and fauna. The age – old heritage and tradition, bright festivals and dances, and elating boat races are among Kerala's prime attractions. Kerala is an epicurean paradise and the Keralian cuisine is one of the cuisine that enjoy worldwide recognition and appreciation, which one can describe as extremely exotic and relishing. Kerala has been influenced by many culinary methods in past which are deeply rooted in the traditional Keralian cuisine in the lives of people. Cooking in Kerala is more than just preparation of food. It is a celebration of the rich culture that is deeply imbued in the life of Keralian. This south Indian state that cradles between Western Ghats and Arabian Sea swings between juicy seafood and aromatic traditional dishes. It is indeed true that the geography culture and to some extent history play an important role in giving the cuisine of Kerala some unforgettable flavour. Kerala cuisine is famous for its mouthwatering recipes and authentic Malayali dishes. Kerala food is spicy and delectable. Kerala has its own distinctive cuisine using the ingredients locally available.

Sea food is popular among Malayalis. The evolution of the culinary style of Kerala can be traced to the society, culture, history and topography of the state.

Karnataka:

The cuisine of **Karnataka** as any other Indian cuisine, is influenced by both Hindu and Muslim traditions brought by the different rulers of this region. The culinary fare offered by Karnataka is quite varied with each region of the state having its own unique flavour. Many factors and influences have contributed to enrich this culinary heritage. Though there are many similarities between the food of Karnataka and its southern neighbours, the typical Mysore cuisine is well known for its own distinctive textural forms and flavour with the dishes complementing and balancing each other.

CHAPTER TWO

Bird's Eye View of the South Indian Cuisine

South Indian cuisine is rice based. Rice is combined with lentils to make wonderful dosas, idli, vada and uttapams. These items are glorious and delicious besides being nourishing and digestible (due to the fermenting process). They are combined with sambar (Dal) Rasam (tamarind dal) and curried vegetables and Pacchhadi. Their rice preparations are also masterpieces like Biryanis from Hyderabad, lemon rice and rice seasoned with coconut, peanuts, tamarind, chillies, curry leaves, urad dal and fenugreek seeds.

South Indian chutneys are made of tamarind, coconut, peanuts, pulses, fenugreek seeds and cilantro. Meals are followed by coffee. South Indian dals and curries are soupier than North Indian dals and curries. South Indian cuisine is hotter as well. Coconut milk straight from the nut is a common beverage and site in South India. Coffee is very popular in South India and Madras Coffee is popular in South Indian restaurants throughout the world. The South Indian food is a brilliant blend of flavours, colours, seasoning, nutritional balance, fragrance, taste and visual appeal.

"Parimaral - The South Indian tradition of serving a traditional meal or a typical traditional meal. A typical traditional meal in South India is served as a 'vazhaillai', a freshly cut plantation leaf or a banana leaf, even the size of the leaf differs from one community to another, it is displays like an identity card, one look and the guest will know the community the status the exact wealth of the family and from where they originate."

The top half of the leaf is reserved for accessories, the lower half for the rice. In some communities the rice will be served only after the guest has been seated. The lower right portion of the leaf may have a scoop of warm sweet milk rice 'payasam' which should be slurped up quickly while the top left includes a pinch of salt, a dash of pickle, and thumb full salad and chutney. In the middle of the leaf there may be an odd number of fried items like small circles of chips of either banana or potato, hard round discs of spiced ground Dal known as thin Papad or Wafers or vada. Top right hand corner is reserved for the heavy artillery.

The curries, hot sweet or sour and dry items if it is a vegetarian meal. The vegetables are carefully chosen between the country ones like guards, drumsticks, brinjals, and the English ones like carrot, cabbage and cauliflower. If it is a non vegetarian meal, in some cases, a separate leaf is provided for the fried meats, chicken, fish, crab, and so on. But again, the variations are presented carefully, one dry next to a gravied one.

There may be a side attraction such as a 'puran poli' (sweetened dal stuffed into a pancake), puri, sweet rice, or any one of the famed rice preparations like Bisi Bele bhat. After having worked through the preliminaries, the long haul starts with the rice which is generally doused with ghee, sambar, the highly spiced Dal based dish containing whatever appropriate seasonal vegetables, follows and this is succeeded buy rasam. Final round of rice and curd or buttermilk for both a traditional meal concludes with a small banana, a few leaves of betel and nuts.

The foundations of South Indian Cuisine:

Rice – Saadham:

Rice is the staple food and is divided into three basic categories.

- Long white Grain Rice – most commonly used.
- Short Grain Rice – used to make sweet dishes.
- Round Grain Rice – for worshipping.

Lentil – Paruppu:

Paruppu (dal/lentil) is the mainspring of the common man's diet. Every meal includes Paruppu. It may be made a soup, chutney, spicy powder, sambhar, snacks and sweets.

South Indian meal courses:

Sweet in Ayurveda is considered to be an appetite builder. Taking its cues from Ayurveda the South Indian meal would generally begin with _e-ne-ip-pu_ or sweet. It may consist of the popular _Mysore pak_ (gram flour fudge).

The three courses of Rice:

Rice with Sambar: There are many forms of rice such as the plain rice – ghee – boiled lentil (_sadam-neai-paruppu)_ , coconut rice, lemon rice, tamarind rice.

Rice with Rasam: Rasam is a tangy, spicy, watery and soupy tamarind concoction which is served rice.

Curd Rice: This is served last to cool the mouth and the digestive system. It may be served with non spicy assorted vegetable dishes, namely the _aviyal_ (mixed vegetable stew), _Kari_ (dry masala vegetable) and _kootu_ (coconut and vegetable saute'ate' which are not too wet and not too dry).

> "_Finally the palpayasam (Milk sweet) a dessert, is served._
> _After the meal, paan or betel nut, which freshens the mouth and aids digestion._ "

Culinary Schools of South Indian cuisine:

(Telugu, Hyderabadi, Tamil-Chettinad, and Kerala)
Andhra – Andhra cuisine is largely vegetarian but the coastal areas have a large repertoire of seafood. Fish and prawns are curried in sesame and coconut oils, and flavoured with freshly ground pepper. Andhra food is served with rice, sambhar and other lentils preparations, and steamed vegetables delicately flavoured with coconut, spices and fresh herbs. Snacks

or Tiffin are made of many preparations like Onion Pakoras, Vadas dunked in sambhar, and steamed rice muffins called idlis. Savouries are *murukku*, roundels of rice flour paste deep fried and pappadums. Desserts include payasam, a pudding made with rice and milk and the popular Sheer Khurma of Hyderabad.

Hyderabadi Cuisine is a direct result from the kitchens of the Nizams or Muslim Rulers. The Hyderabadi cuisine is the meeting of the muslim techniques of meat cooking with the spices and masalas used by the predominantly hindu population of the region. Hyderabadi cuisine is the ultimate in fine dining. Its taste ranges from sour to the sweet, the hot & savoury to the ones studded with dry fruits and nuts. One of India's finest foods, the *biryani* with mutton or chicken and the *Baghare Baingan* (egg plants/ brinjal based delicacy).

Tamil Nadu – Chettinad cuisine hails from the deep southern regions of Tamil Nadu. Chettinad cookery id far cry from the other wise bland cookery of the traditional Tamil Brahmin households. Chettinad cookery is one of the spiciest, oiliest and yet the most aromatic and addictive to Indian food lovers. Although the Chettiars are well known for their delicious vegetarian preparations, the non vegetarian preparations are as much sought after. Fish and fowl meats, as well as delicate noodle-like dishes carefully preserved sun-dried legumes and berries that the Chettiar ladies make into curries. Oil and spices are liberally used in cooking and most dishes have generous amounts of peppercorns, chillies, bay leaves, cardamom, nutmeg, green and red chillies, etc. Some popular dishes in the chettinad menu would be *varuval* – a dry dish fried with onions and spices (chicken, fish, or vegetables sautéed), pepper Chicken. *Poriyal* – a curry, and *kuzhambu* which has the ingredients stewed in a gravy of coconut milk and spices.

Kerala is noted for its variety of pancakes and steamed rice cakes made from pounded rice. For the Muslims, the lightly flavoured Biryani made of mutton, chicken, eggs, or fish takes pride. In seafood mussels are everyone's favourite. For the Christians, who can be seen in large concentrations in areas like Kottayam and Pala, *Ishtew* (a derivation of the European stew), with *appam* is a must for every marriage reception. Kerala also has its own fermented beverage – the famous *Kallu* (Toddy) and *Patta Charayam* (arrack). Arrack is extremely intoxicating and is usually consumed with spicy pickles and boiled eggs (*patta and mutta*).

CHAPTER THREE

Andhra Cuisine

Introduction to Andhra:

> *"Andhra Pradesh is one of the south Indian states and is positioned in the coastal area towards the south eastern part of the country and because of its location in the merging area of the Deccan plateau and the coastal plains and also transverse by Krishna and Godavari rivers, the state experiences varied physical features."*

This typical topography of the state enables it acquire rich and heterogeneous culture and heritage. Being ruled by some of the famous dynasties in the historical times, this south Indian state is said to have a rich cultural heritage. Historically the state is known as the — *Rice Bowl of India.* Andhra cuisine or Telugu cuisine is a cuisine of South India native to the Telugu people from the states of Andhra Pradesh and Telangana. Generally known for its tangy, hot and spicy taste, the cooking is very diverse due to the vast spread of the people and varied topological regions.

Geography:

Andhra Pradesh is one of the 29 states of India. Situated in the south – east of the country, it is the seventh – largest state in India. The state is made up of the two major regions of Rayalaseema, in the inland southwestern part of the state, and Coastal Andhra to the east and northeast, bordering the Bay of Bengal. The state also boasts of having the second longest coastline in India, which stretches up to 970 km. The state is bordered by Telangana in the north – west, Chhattisgarh and Odisha in the north – east, Karnataka in the west, Tamil Nadu in the south, and to the east lies the Bay of Bengal.

The north – western portion of Andhra Pradesh was separated to form the new state of Telangana on 2 June 2014, and Hyderabad, the longtime capital of Andhra Pradesh, was transferred to Telangana as part of the division. Presently Amravati has been announced the Capital of the state of Andhra Pradesh. The entire state is divided into the following 3 distinct regions: Telangana Region, Rayalaseema Region and Coastal Andhra Region. Godavari, Krishna, Pennar and Tungabhadra are the four major rivers that pass through this state. The northern side of the Deccan plateau is marked as the Telangana region, while the southern side is known as the Rayalaseema region. River Krishna separates these two regions from each other. The coastal area of the state is mostly formed by the deltas of these rivers of Andhra Pradesh. Apart from these major rivers, there are around 17 other rivers and streams flowing through Andhra Pradesh whose basins cover almost 75% of the state territory.

Andhra Pradesh possesses many hills that run intermittently, separating the state into western and eastern (coastal) Andhra. The hill ranges like Simhachalam, Annavaram, Srisailam and Tirumalai – Tirupati, have become the integral geographical part of states life and history.

History:

Andhra Pradesh's history dates back to the Vedic period and is said to have been the home of the Pre – Dravidian inhabitants. The earliest mention of the Andhras was mentioned in the Aitareya Brahmana and it was called Dakshina Pandit during those days. It has mention in the famous Indian epics Mahabharata, Ramayana, the Jataka Tales and the Puranas.

The glorious past of Andhra Pradesh is a result of the many different dynasties that have ruled the region. The influence of the rulers on the culture and tradition of this south Indian state have been immense. This state located in the Godavary valley witnessed absolute political power during the reign of Chandragupta Maurya of Mauryan dynasty.

Historical evidence proves that between 624 AD and 1323 AD a significant change in social, religious and the literary fields were brought about. The identity of Andhra Pradesh as an established region was brought about during the reign of the Satvahanas, Ikshvakus, Pallavas, Chalukya's, the Rashtrakutas and the Cholas. During the 12th and 13th century the Kakatiya dynasty ruled the empire and developed culturally.

In 1370 the administration of the region was overtaken by the Vijayanagar Empire. The last Hindu empire it spread in size and strengthened its position easily. The dynasty was founded by Hukka and Bukka and reached its pinnacle of glory at a very early stage. In 1323 CE, Ghiaz – ud – din Tughlaq captured Warangal, with the assistance of Ulugh Khan and established the Kutub dynasty, which ruled for 200 years and witnessed the rise of the independent Muslim power in the region.

In 1518 the Sultan Qili Qutub Shah declared himself independent and founded the Qutub Shah dynasty which existed till 1687. During this period literature, art and architect are advanced. The city of Hyderabad was laid in 1591 by Muhammad Quli Qutub Shah. The Mughals put an end to the Qutub Shahi rule in 1687. After this the Asafjahis called Nizams emerged. They influenced Andhra Pradesh till the 18th century till Andhra Pradesh was ceded to the East India Company who named it Rayalaseema.

Gradually the whole of Andhra Pradesh except Hyderabad was under the British till 1947. The Nizams still controlled the princely state of Hyderabad. In 1947, India became free from the clutches of the British. The Muslim Nizam of Hyderabad preferred to be independent from India; however Hyderabad was enforced to become part of the Republic of India in 1948. Andhra state was merged with the Telugu speaking area of Telangana and Andhra Pradesh was created in 1965. In February 2014 both chambers of the Indian parliament gave approval for the division of Andhra state and creation of Telangana state, which became India's 29th state on June 2.

Culture and Tradition:

The Andhras are also known as Telugu. Their traditional home is the land between the Godavari and Kistna (Krishna) rivers in southeastern India. Today, Andhras are the dominant group in the state of Andhra Pradesh. They have a concoction of various communities, religions, customs, lifestyles and cultures. In broad terms, the people of Andhra are nice and friendly, who live in perfect harmony, in spite of belonging to different castes and following different religions. They are highly pious people, who follow their religion with the highest regard.

In Andhra Pradesh, the major religions are Hinduism, Islam, Christianity and Buddhism. Around the state, you can find people following different religious practices, along with their own notions and customs. Hero worship is important in Andhra culture. Andhra warriors who died on the battlefield or who sacrificed their lives for great or pious causes are worshiped as gods. The state is dominated by Hindus.

The Brahman castes (priests and scholars) have the highest social status, and Brahmans serve as priests in temples. Andhras worship Shiva, Vishnu, Hanuman, and other Hindu gods. Andhras also worship Ammas or village goddesses. Durgamma presides over the welfare of the village, Maisamma protects the village boundaries, and Balamma is a goddess of fertility. These deities are all forms of the Mother Goddess and play a big role in daily life. These deities often have priests drawn from the lower castes, and low castes may use their own priests rather than Brahmans.

The areas especially in and around Hyderabad there is a significantly large population of Muslims. The richest sections of Andhra society are the Raos and the Reddys. These landowning classes with a penchant for flashy lifestyles dominate the social scene in cities like Hyderabad. While urban Andhra Pradesh is educated, cosmopolitan and leads the way in conspicuous consumerism, the rural areas are still remarkably poor and lead agricultural lifestyle.

> *"A typical house is square in shape and is built around a courtyard. The walls are made of stone, the floor is made of mud, and the roof is tiled. There are two or three rooms, used for living, sleeping, and housing livestock. One room is used for the family shrine and to keep valuables. The doors are often carved, and designs are painted on the walls. Most houses lack toilets, the inhabitants using the fields for their natural functions. There may be a backyard used for growing vegetables and keeping chickens. Furnishings consist of beds, wooden stools, and chairs. Kitchen utensils are usually of earthenware and are made by the village potters."*

Climate:

The state has a tropical climate. Summer lasts from March to June, a season of tropical rains that runs from July to September, and a winter lasts from October to February constitute the three seasons of Andhra Pradesh. Summers are extraordinarily hot and humid, with maximum daily temperatures exceeding 35 °C and even surpassing 40 °C in the central portion of the state. Winters are somewhat cooler, with January maximum temperatures between 30 and 35 °C in all but the northeastern portion of the state. Winter lows drop below about 15 °C only in the extreme northeast.

The state is principally fed by the southwest monsoon while the northeast monsoon contributes about one – third of rainfall. Coastal areas receive about 40 to 47 inches per year, while the westernmost part of the plateau may receive only half that much. Rainfall totals in portions of the northeastern mountains exceed 47 inches and can be as high as 55 inches. The east coast region has been prone to disastrous cyclonic storms, which have destroyed much life and the livelihood of the villagers in the area.

Staple Food:

Agriculture is the backbone of the economic structure of Andhra Pradesh. Most of the people of the state are cultivators who earn their living by cultivating the lands of their forefathers. Andhra Pradesh is historically called the Rice Bowl of India. The State has a large river system which supplements the rainfall in the State. It is one of the few States in the country blessed with riverine geography. Agriculture is the main occupation of about 62 per cent of the people in Andhra Pradesh.

Rice is the major food crop and staple food of the state contributing about 77 per cent of the food grain production which almost accounts for 25 per cent of the state's gross cropped area. Andhra Pradesh was among the very few states in the country which went in for the *Green Revolution* in rice cultivation in the 1970s. Other important crops are jowar, bajra, maize, ragi, small millets, pulses, castor, tobacco, cotton and sugarcane etc. Four important rivers of India, the Godavari, Krishna, Penna, and Tungabhadra flow through the state, providing irrigation. Recently, crops used for vegetable oil production such as sunflower and peanuts have gained favour.

There are many multi – state irrigation projects in development, including Godavari River Basin Irrigation Projects and Nagarjuna Sagar Dam. The state also produces other important cash crops like Groundnut, Pulses, Castor, Sunflower, Cotton, Oilseeds, and Sugarcane which helps the state to earn huge amounts of revenue. Andhra Pradesh is also an important producer of horticulture crops. Mango, banana, grapes, papaya, guava, brinjal, cabbage, chillies and turmeric are the main horticultural produce. Aquaculture such as cultivating fish, crustaceans, mollusks, shrimp production etc. is the major occupations of coastal areas. Andhra Pradesh is the largest producer of shrimp in the country, with 70% of the production from the state itself.

Features of the Andhra (Telugu) Cuisine:

The cuisine of Andhra is based mostly on regional variation, its rich cultural heritage and the influence of the Royal recipes from the Nawabs. The cuisine of Andhra Pradesh is mixed between the eating habits of the Hindus and Muslims style of eating.

The influence of external powers has influenced every aspect of the Andhra society. From music, dance, cuisine and literature, the foreign powers have left a mark of their own. This variety and diversity has helped the culture to become richer and more successful. The Nawabs and Sultans who ruled over the Deccan brought some of the best cooks from all over the country to make the Deccan the food capital. So much so that when you talk of Andhra or its capital, Hyderabad, visions of a mouth – watering biryani comes to mind.

If there is any one statement that can, in a nutshell, describe the Andhra kitchen, it is: Andhra food is hot! Local legend says that there was once severe famine in the area and all that grew, and grew well, was chillies – red chillies, famous in a place called Guntur in Andhra. So people made as many dishes as possible with chillies. A more realistic explanation comes from nutritionists who say that being a very hot area, there are more chances of stomach infection for the local people. They probably make use of large quantities of chillies to guard against stomach infection. A parallel can be found in the desert state of Rajasthan in northern India.

The cuisine of Andhra Pradesh can be broadly classified into 4 regions:

- Kosta (Circar)
- Hyderabad
- Rayalaseema
- Telangana

Kosta (Circar) –

The Coastal Andhra region is dominated by Krishna and Godavari delta regions and is exposed to the long coastline of Bay of Bengal. Hence the recipes mainly consist of rice, dal and seafood. This region has its own variations, but ultimately the dishes are predominantly rice – based and sweeter in taste and they often cook lentils in jaggary (referred to as *Bellam Pappu*) enjoyed with butter and steamed rice. This region is one of the largest producers of rice and chilies. The coastal region is endowed with plenty of natural resources; hence the cooking and preserving methods are highly sophisticated. *Ulava charu* is a famous soup made from horse gram; *Bommidala Pulusu* is a fish stew that is a specialty of this region. They cook vegetables in gravies of *menthipettina kura* (fenugreek seed paste), *avapettina kura* (mustard seed paste), *nuvvugunda kura* (sesame paste), etc.

Hyderabad –

Also known as *Deccani* of *Nizami* cuisine, is the native culinary art of the Hyderabadi Muslims. This is an amalgamation of Mughlai, Arabic, and Turkish delicacies, blended with native Maratha and Telugu culinary traditions; it subsequently became a royal legacy of the Nizams, the erstwhile rulers of the State of Hyderabad. The cuisine, mainly comprising of rice, wheat, and meat dishes prepared with various natural edibles, spices, and herbs, has different recipes for different occasions. It is broadly classified into banquet foods, festival foods, travel foods, and foods for weddings and parties. *Jahaji Korma*—a spiced meat delicacy—for example, derives its name from _Jahaj‘, which means a ship, and can be categorized as a travel food meant to be carried for long – distance journeys. Another popular non – vegetarian dish are the ‘Kababs’, which is meat pieces or minced meat cooked in many different styles such as ‘Boti Jhammi’, ‘Kalmi’, ‘Shikampur’, ‘Sheek’, ‘Lagan – ke – Kababs’, ‘Dum – ke – kababs’. ‘Kormas’ is yet another preparation which is either meat or vegetables cooked in rich with creamy gravy and ‘Lukhmi’, a pastry. The cuisine boasts for its biriyani world over. Unlike the biriyanis of Lucknow where all the ingredients are mixed together and put to Dum (*Pakki biriyani*), the Hyderabadi biriyani is prepared with all the material in raw state cooked together in Dum style to perfection (*Kachchi biriyani*). They have also adopted foods from different countries and molded them in their own style, like Biryani and *Asaf Jahi Kebab* is from Turkey, *til – ki – chutney* and *Haleem* is from Saudi Arabia, *Dalcha* and *Lukmi* from Persia and *Sheermal* from Uzbekistan. They also adopted and developed accordingly to their taste many dishes from their

Mughlal counterparts of north India like *Sheer Korma*, Chicken Korma, *Bina Masale Ka Murgh*, or *Gajar – ka – halwa, Dum Ke Baingan*, Colocasia Curry, *Mirch – Ka – Salan*, and *Bagaara Baingan*, *sheermal*, *Double Ka Meetha* (Shahi tukda of Mughlai*)*, '*Qubani – ka – Meetha*' (stewed apricot dessert); '*Ande – ka – Piyosi*' (made with eggs, almonds and purified butter); '*Badam – ki – Jhab*' (marzipan) and '*Dil – e – Firdaus*' (a rich, milk – based sweet)..

Rayalaseema -

Rayalaseema has its own culinary delights. It is influenced mainly by Tamil Nadu and south Karnataka cuisine. Due to the region's dry and arid areas, the level of pungency and spice is highest in the world. Vegetarian as well as meat and seafood (coastal areas) feature prominently in the menus. Lentils, tomato and tamarind are largely used for cooking curries. Popular dishes from the Rayalaseema regions are the *Alsandala vada, Ulavacharu, Peetala Kura, Brain fry, Liver fry* and *Prawn Iguru* which can be combined with Sajja or Jonna rotis and Raagi sankati (a very healthy and nutritious food) etc. *Attirasaalu* or *Aresalu* (rice – based fritter using jaggary), *Badeshi, Jaagiri, Jilebi, Pakam Undalu* (mixture of steam rice flour, ground nuts, jaggery), *Borugu Undalu* (a sweet variety made corn of jowar and jaggery), *Pala Kova, Rava Laddu* are few of the mouth watering sweets also known as *Bakshalu* of this region. The "*Naatu Kodi Biryani*" is hotter than the usual Biryani.

Telangana –

Telangana is known for its distinctive cuisine that includes a wide variety of sweet and savoury dishes. Being a semi – arid state, the staple food in Telangana is not rice but sorghum and millet breads. The food in this region is spicy and hot due to inclusion of red chillies. On the other hand, due to the Islamic dynasties reigning over centuries, the Telangana region has a distinct Mughlai flavor. In the Telugu cuisine of the Telangana region, meats play a dominating role. Popular vegetarian dishes from the land of Telangana are the *Ulli akku kura* (spring onion curry), *Kakaraya pulusu* (gravy made of bitter gourd), *pesarattu pulusu, rasam, Karapu Annam* (Chilli rice) etc. The famous non – vegetarian dishes are *Chapala Pulusu* (fish gravy), *Kodi Kura, Guddu Pulusu* (also known as Egg Pulusu), Meat curry, Shrimp curry, etc. Famous snacks of the Telangana region are the *Billavakka* (snack prepared with rice flour and deep fried), *Sakinalu* – a traditional snack usually prepared during Sankranti festival made of rice flour and sesame seeds. Common breakfast includes *Sarva Pindi* (a flatbread made of a mixture of various flours flecked with peanuts, coriander, chillies, garlic, ginger, sesame seeds and chana dal). Sweets include *Kobbari Pappu Payasam (moong dal cooked in milk and grated coconut)* and *Garijelu* (deep fried dumpling with a sweet coconut and sugar filling inside).

Common characteristics -

- Rice is the staple food of the region.
- The cuisine of Andhra Pradesh is mostly vegetarian but the coastal areas have a vast repertoire of seafood preparations.
- Fish and Prawns are major seafood eaten here. They are mainly found with curry in sesame and coconut oils along with grounded pepper flavor and are eaten with rice.
- Biriyanis are mostly cooked using raw materials cooked altogether in dum style to perfection using secret spices which are prepared and passed on through *Ustad* (Chef/cook) to his *Shagird* (pupil).
- Red chillies are predominantly used in the cuisine making it one of the hottest and spiciest. The chillies grow well in the Guntur region.
- Pickles are an essential part of the cuisine and the variety is countless. Podis, a mixture of various ingredients which are dried or broiled and powdered, are as important as pickle. These homemade podis are sprinkled over rice, and a dollop of pure ghee is offered, which is also mixed with the podi and rice and eaten.
- Gongura is an edible plant grown in India. It is a species of the Sorrel leaves. *Gongura pachadi* is quintessentially Telugu cuisine along with pacchadi (chutney or relish). While it has many culinary uses, the most popular is the pickled version. Although Gongura is widely consumed all over Andhra Pradesh, Guntur Gongura is more popular. Gongura is a very rich source of Iron, vitamins, folic acid and anti – oxidants essential for human nutrition. It is a summer crop, and the hotter the place, the more sour the leaf gets.
- Modati Mudda / Starter – Rice with some podi, khaaram, or a certain variety of pickles and ghee is eaten as the modati mudda (the first bite). Modati mudda items tend to taste sour or hot, have strong aromas, and include ingredients with medicinal values, such as dry ginger and curry leaves. They are usually intended to stimulate appetite and aid digestion.
- Pappu – Toor Daal (Kandi Pappu) or Moong Daal (Pesara pappu) cooked with a vegetable or green. No masala is added to the dal. Some regions

include garlic and onion in the seasoning while some regions prefer asafetida (hing/Inguva).

- Pachadi / Ooragaya – For a typical Andhrite, no meal is complete without this very essential item. It is consumed on its own mixed with rice and is also eaten as a side dish with pappu / koora. There are two broad varieties – Pachadi (chutney) is typically made of vegetables/ greens and roasted green/ red chillies. It is prepared fresh and is consumed within a day or two. *Ooragaya* is prepared in massive amounts seasonally and uses liberal amounts of chilli powder, methi (fenugreek) powder, mustard powder and oil.
- Light Bite – The range of snack is also quite good here. Some of the snacks that can be enjoyed here are onion *'Pakodas'*, *'Vadas'*, *'Murku'* (roundels of rice flour that are deep fried), and *'Appadams'*. Some of the desserts that are a part of this cuisine are, *'Putharekulu'*, *'Kakinada Kaja'*, *'Bobbatlu'*, *'Booralu'*, and *'Bandhar Ladoo'*.

Other ingredients used the cuisine are:

- Cowpeas (*Bobbarlu*): This is also known as black eyed beans or lobiya in northern India. It can be stewed or can be braised with spices.
- Field beans (*Chikkudu*): These beans are from the family of Broad beans. They are used fresh and even the leaves are eaten curried.
- Agathi leaves (*Avise*): These are classified under green leafy vegetables. The plant that produces white flowers are suitable for eating while those producing red flowers are not.
- Sorrel leaves (*Chukka koora*): These resembles spinach but has a slightly sour taste. The sour flavour of the leaves combine well with the spices used in the Andhra cuisine.
- Banana rhizome (*Arati dumpa*): The rhizome or the roots of the banana plant is often used in stir – fried dishes or even in curries.
- Spine gourd (*Akakara*): It resembles bitter gourd in shape but is not as bitter. It is used in sambhars or curries in Andhra cuisine.
- Cudapa seeds or chironji or chaoroli nuts (*Sara Pappu*): These are nuts that are used as a thickening agent.

- Zizyphus (*Regu pandu*): These are a type of jujubes and are extensively used in pickles and chutneys. The dried Regu pandu is often crushed with red chillies, jiggery and tamarind and used in curries.

Andhra Speciality Food List:

1. Dhaniyala karappodi: Roasted chillies ground with coriander seeds.
2. Allam: Ginger
3. Allam khaaram: Ginger ground with raw or roasted red and green chillies.
4. Avakaya: Green mango pickle
5. Chepa: Fish
6. Chintakaya: Chutney made of grounded tamarind seeds, salt and red chillies
7. Chuppulu: Chakli's made using rice flour, sesame seeds, ajwain
8. Dabbakaya: jackfruit
9. Dabbakaya pachadi: Jackfruit sauce
10. Karam: Various types of dry powders make from lentils or chillies, eaten with ghee.
11. Karivepaku karappodi: Roasted chillies and curry leaves.
12. Karivepaku khaaram: Curry leaves ground with raw or roasted red chillies.
13. Killi: Pan
14. Kodi: Chicken
15. Koora: Curry
16. Korivi Khaaram: Spicy sauce made of ground red chillies, tamarind and salt.
17. Kottimeera khaaram: Cilantro leaves ground with raw or roasted red chillies.
18. Kottimeera: Green coriander
19. Magaya: Ripe mango pickle
20. Majjiga Pulusu: Buttermilk cooked with turmeric and boiled vegetables.
21. Mudda pappu: Plain toor dal cooked with salt
22. Neeti kaya: Avakaya made by grinding mustard paste with water
23. Nimmakaya: Lime marinade made with salt, methi powder and chilli powder.

24. Nuvvula podi: Sesame seeds ground with roasted chillies.
25. Ooragaya: Pickle
26. Pachadi: Pickles or raita or chutney
27. Pachimirapakaya khaaram: Roasted and ground green chillies.
28. Pappu: Dal
29. Peethal: Crab
30. Perugu: Curd
31. Ponganalu: Fried batter puffs
32. Royyalu: Prawn
33. Shonthi podi: Dry ginger ground with a pinch of salt.
34. Ullipakodi: Fritters made with sliced onion and spices in chickpea batter.
35. Usirikaya: Sauce made by grinding goose berries, salt and red chillies.
36. Usirikaya pachadi: Pickled Indian gooseberries typically mixed with roasted red chillies or chili powder.

Equipments and Utensils:

- Chippa: This is a clay pot that is wok – shaped and is used for cooking chippa gosth – a lamb dish that gets its name from this equipment.
- Tathee: This is a metal stand similar to a bar – be – que griller, which is placed on smouldering charcoals to grill kebab.
- Tiragali: This is a stone mill that is used grinding rice to a perfect consistency foe certain desserts such as adhirsam. Too fine a powder would make the dessert too sticky to eat and too coarse a powder would not allow it to shape properly.
- Kavam: This is a kind of churner used for churning buttermilk – it is nearly similar to a whisk. It is manually twisted between the palms for churning the liquid food, for example – churning of yoghurt for making buttermilk.
- Ponganalu: This equipment is made up of cast iron and is used for making a dish called ponganalu, which is eaten for breakfast. It has round depressions into which a batter of rice and dal is poured and cooked over fire.
- Jaadilu: These are traditional pickle jars used to store home – made pickles. These are made from ceramic as it does not react with pickles.

- Rolu / Pothram: This is a stone mortar and pestle and is used for grinding whole spices and making chutneys.
- Kancham : broad steel food plates
- Vistari – Plantain leaf plate.
- Katti – vegetable knife

Festive Speciality Dishes:

1. Burani raita: It is a creamy raita from the Hyderabadi cuisine, which is very easy and quick to prepare and pairs perfectly with spicy biryanis. This raita is not only refreshing but is packed with the flavours too. This raita has hints of garlic and roasted cumin powder.
2. Palathalikalu: Rice flour is made into a very thick batter which is pushed through small holes into boiling milk and simmered for a long time to achieve a thick consistency.
3. Pappu koora: Boiled vegetables stir – fried with a small amount of half – cooked lentils (dal).
4. Chepa pulusu: A variety of hot piquant fish curry dish, in which fish is tossed in tamarind sauce and assorted with spicy flavorings.
5. Bobbatlu: It is a popular Indian sweet prepared with maida (all-purpose flour) stuffed with mashed chana dal mixed with jaggery. It is similar to puran poli of Maharashtra.
6. Bongu kodi: The marinated chicken is stuffed into a fresh green bamboo and cooked in live coal. The heat penetrates the bamboo and then it makes the chicken tender, the nutrition's, flavour and taste is completely retained in the dish.
7. Boorelu: A mixture of boiled chana dal, jaggery, elaichi, ghee, coated in rice flour batter & deep fried.
8. Challa pulusu: Sour buttermilk boiled with channa dal and coconut paste.
9. Chapa vepudu: One of commonest recipes of Andhra Pradesh, Chapa vepudu is a spicy, marinated fish fry. Chapa means fish in Telugu, and this fried murrel fish preparation has been an evergreen choice for the admirers of the Telugu cuisine.
10. Charu: A very dilute concoction of tamarind and charu podi (made of coriander seeds, dal, ginger, pepper and hing). It is also taken as such

during the meal like a soup without mixing with rice.

11. Dondakaya fry: The Dondakaya fry is a stir fry item, prepared with ivy gourd curry, also known as parwal, kundru, and tindli in other languages of the country.

12. Double ka meetha: It is a delicious dessert recipe which is popularly made on the day of Eid. It is made using bread slices and reduced milk and is loaded with dry fruits for a delicious crunch.

13. Garijalu (kajjikayalu): A traditional sweet that is prepared by rolling out small balls of maida dough into thin puris and filled with a mixture of dry coconut, sugar, semolina and cardamom powder and deep fried. Similar to gujia of Uttar Pradesh.

14. Gavvalu: Shell shaped sweets made using rice flour,ghee, jaggery, milk.

15. Gonghuraa pachadi: Also known as gongura chutney. Gongura leaves which are further spiced up with coriander, cumin, fenugreek and mustard seeds. The mix is well ground to make chutney with thick consistency. It is a signature dish of Andhra Pradesh

16. Gongura pickle ambadi: Fiery spicy pickle made with ambadi leaves, otherwise known as sorrel leaves.

17. Gosht pasinde: Gosht pasinde is one of the most classic and popular Hyderabadi dishes, that is loved in equal measure by locals and tourists alike. The dish has thick gravy, shallow fried vegetables along with moist chunks of meat. French beans and potatoes are most popularly used in Gosht Pasinde but you can find preparations with different seasonal vegetables.

18. Gutti vankaya koora: Eggplant stuffed with roasted spicy herbs and seasonings to give to a perfect delicious taste.

19. Haleem: It is a type of stew popular in Hyderabad. It is a stew composed of meat, lentils and pounded wheat made into a thick paste. Most popular during Ramzan.

20. Hyderabadi marag: It is a soup recipe made with tender mutton attached to bones which has been getting quite popular in Hyderabad. The soup has become one of the starters at Hyderabadi weddings.

21. Jantikalu: Long streaks of *sev* made using gram flour, rice flour and salt, turmeric, chilli powder, and deep fried.

22. Kaaram petti koora / koora podi koora: Sauteed vegetables cooked with curry powder or paste, served as a solid mass. The vegetables can be stuffed with curry powder or paste and are usually cooked whole.

23. Kakinada khaja: Is a sweet preparation made using, wheat flour, refined wheat flour, rice flour, ghee, which is made into flaky rectangles and soaked in sugar syrup

24. Keema samosa: Keema samosa is a popular road side snack recipe which is deep fried and delicious. This snack recipe is made using mutton keema and maida. It is ideal for snacks and occasion like kitty party.

25. Khajalu: It is a sweet preparation made using, refined wheat flour, rice flour, ghee, which is made into flaky rectangles and soaked in sugar syrup.

26. Kharam pulusu: Any vegetable cooked in much diluted tamarind juice and Pulusu Podi (made of roast red chillies, coriander powder).

27. Khatti dal: It is a very popular dal recipe mainly made in Hyderabad which is a tangy tamarind tomato dal and often accompanied with kebabs or koftas as side dishes.

28. Kobbari pulao: An exotic version of coconut rice, also known as Kobbari pulao, is enriched with flavour of coconut. The main ingredients are rice and coconut. Kobbari pulao finds its place in kitchens often during festivities and special gatherings.

29. Kothimira annam: This is a coriander rice dish.

30. Kothimiri kodi: This is a chicken curry form the telugu cuisine. This Andhra chicken curry preparation made by using coriander leaves paste. Kotimira means coriander and kodi means chicken in Telugu.

31. Kubani ka meetha: Or Qubani Ka Meetha is an authentic Hyderabadi delicacy made with dried apricots and is a traditional dessert often served during occasions like weddings and gatherings.

32. Lukhmi: It is a typical mince savoury or starter of the cuisine of Hyderabad. It is usually a flat square shaped flour parcel with a flaky and crisp upper crust and stuffed with beef or mutton – based filling.

33. Maghaz masala: This spicy brain fry is a famous lamb dish from Hyderabad. The thick, fiery gravy with juicy meat is a must try for every non – veg lover.

34. Medu vada: Known with a variety of names like Ulundu Vadai, Ulli Garelu and Uzhunnu Vada, the delicious doughnut – like savoury is prepared widely during all festivals and celebrations. The main ingredient is the urad dal,

35. Menthi challa / menthi majjiga: Sour buttermilk seasoned with ginger / green chili paste and methi seeds fried in oil.

36. Minapattu: These are spicy and crispier dosas like masala dosa, rava dosa, sada dosa, and rava masala dosa

37. Mirchi ka salan: Or curried chilli peppers is a delicious, complex and classic dish originally from Hyderabad, but relished all over the country. Large green chillies are cooked in tamarind, peanuts and spices which instead of heightening the spice, works well to create a beautiful blend of tastes.

38. Mutton dalcha: It is made with meat or mutton mixed in bottle gourd it is made with mutton, chana dal and a host of spices. . It is the most common dish made in Hyderabad which has been passing on since the Nizam's era.

39. Nelluru chepalapulusu: A variety of fish curry, popularly known as Chepapulusu in the state of Andhra is a hot piquant dish with fish tossed in tamarind sauce and assorted with spicy flavourings and tamarind juice to give it a die – for taste.

40. Paaya: It is a soup served at various festivals and gatherings, or made for special guests. Paaya means trotters of goat, sheep or beef. The chopped trotters are stewed with herbs and spices.

41. Pachi pulusu: Unheated version of the pulusu. It includes finely chopped raw onions in a very dilute tamarind juice with jaggery. In the summer season when mangos are abundant, tamarind is replaced by stewed raw mango. It is mostly consumed during the hot season.

42. Pesarattu: Pesarattus are similar to dosas, but the batter is made of green mung beans. It is thin and crispy, usually topped with chopped onions, green chillies, ginger pieces, and coriander. It is generally eaten with ginger chutney.

43. Pootharekekulu: The one and only signature dish of east Godavari district. This dish is prepared with rice flour batter and cooked on the special pot in low heat. It come like thin sheet of paper and then it is stuffed with sugar powder or jaggery, nuts and rolled.

44. Pulihora: An exotic version of tamarind rice, also known as Chitrannam, Pulihora, Puliyodhara or Puliyodharai is enriched with spicy flavours to give it a sour and salty taste at the same time. One of the main ingredients is tamarind along with curry leaves, tomatoes, and mustard seeds. A festive dish served to people as prasadam.

45. Punugulu: Prepared with idli batter and deep fried till golden brown, the mouth – watering snack is served with coconut ginger chutney for a perfect lip – smacking taste.

46. Qabooli biryani: It is a lentil – based biryani made from split Bengal gram or channa dal. Biryani is a spicy rice dish that is typically made with vegetables and/or meat. This dish is a specialty item from the kitchens of Hyderabad.

47. Sakinalu: A traditional Telangana snack made with homemade rice flour and sesame seeds. It consists of concentric circles made of rice flour dough, spices and fried in oil.

48. Sheer korma: Or sheer korma is a traditional recipe which is a must make for the festival of Eid. It is made using nylon vermicelli cooked in milk and dry fruits. Saffron is added to it for a unique flavour.

49. Talawa gosht: It is a very simple fired meat preparation with lamb, onion, and basic flavorings originating from Hyderabad. It is usually prepared with Mithi dal or Khatti dal, and is eaten with rice.

50. Telangana sakinalu: Dish is made from rice flour. It is traditional and snack of Telangana region. This crispy and tasty dish is made mostly on occasion of Sankranti.

51. Tiyya pulusu: Mild and sweet vegetables like pumpkin or sweet potato cooked in light tamarind juice with jaggery.

52. Ulusu koora / aava petti koora: Boiled vegetables cooked in tamarind sauce and mustard paste.

53. Uppindi: Uppindi or Arisi Upma, as many call it, is a popular rava upma dish

54. Urgai mamsam: Another spicy non – vegetarian recipes of Andhra Pradesh, is *uragai mamsam*, a delicious dish where tender morsels of lamb are cooked to perfection in pickled masala. *Mamsam* means meat in Telugu, and this non – vegetarian preparation has been a trademark dish of the Telugu cuisine.

55. Vepudu: Crispy fried vegetables, typically including Bendakaya (okra), Dondakaya (tindora), Bangaladumpa (potato), and Colocasia (chamadumpa).

Telugu Festivals:

- **Pongal:** This is an important festival native to South India, particularly Andhra pradesh that marks the commencement of the harvest season or the sun's northward movement. Marking the onset of the new season, the Pongal festival is a great way of thanking God by wiping out old clutter and welcoming the year with new crops. The literal translation of the word 'Pongal' means "boiling over" or "spilling over" in Tamil, which in Indian tradition is a way of denoting abundance and prosperity. In this festival, milk is boiled over as a sign of plenty. It is a four day long celebration consisting of Bhogi Pongal, Surya Pongal, Muttu Pongal and Kaanum Pongal. Sweet rice called 'Pongal' is cooked on the festival.

- **Ugadi:** The word Ugadi also known as Yugadi has been derived by combination of two words Yuga meaning age and adi meaning beginning of a new age. This festival is the celebration of Telugu New Year. It falls in the month of April – May. The people wear new clothes, decorate their houses and make sweets on this day. Purampoli or Bhakshya is the special sweet made on this day. People also make festoons with mango leaves (called Torana) and hang them on the doors of the house and also draw colorful patterns on floor called kolamulus or Rangoli.

- **Ganesha or Vinayak Chaturthi:** This is a festival honoring the birthday of Lord Ganesha or God of New beginning, who removes all obstacles and provide wisdom and intelligence. Stretching for ten days, the festival is marked by worshipping the Ganesha with flowers, fruits, leaves, sandal paste, corns, vermilion, payasam, rice milk porridge (kheer), etc. It is celebrated in the month of August/September. The culmination of the festival is marked by the immersion of the idol of Ganesh in the lake.

- **Deccan Festival:** The festival is basically celebrated to rejoice the era of Qutab Shahi. Qutab Shahi rulers in Hyderabad are believed to be as the great patrons of art and literature of their times. It is a five – day long festival celebrated at Qutub Shahi Tombs in Hyderabad on Second Friday, Saturday and Sunday of April every year. It is dedicated to Hyderabad's arts, crafts, cuisine and culture. It is the most vibrant and enjoyable of all the festivals in Andhra Pradesh. During the festival a food and handicrafts fair is also held.

- **Lumbini Festival:** This three day long Lumbini Festival is an annual festival organized at Nagarjuna Sagar in the state of Andhra Pradesh in the month of December every year. It is a Buddhist festival. The festival is named after the place Lumbini, which is considered the birth place of Gautam Buddha who was the Guru behind Buddhism. Buddhism being once a major religion followed in the state, so to highlight the Buddhist culture and heritage, this festival is organized by the Department of

Tourism of the Government of Andhra Pradesh.

- **Krishna Nandi Festival**: In Kurnool district of Andhra Pradesh, there are some ancient temples at a place like 'Prathama Nandi' and 'Krishna Nandi'. The most important festival here is that of Krishna Nandi celebrated during January – February. This shrine is one of the "Navanandis" in the neighbourhood of Mahanandi and Nandyal. The pilgrims numbering about 50,000 proceeding to Mahanandi from this State as well as Mysore and Maharashtra States, visit this forest shrine during Mahashivaratri.

- **Rayalaseema Food and Dance Festival**: The festival is celebrated to promote the rich heritage, art, culture and cuisine of Andhra Pradesh of the region that dates back to more than 400 years. It is held in the month of October is one of the biggest and most widely celebrated cultural festivals of Andhra Pradesh, particularly Rasyalaseema region of Tirupati in Chitoor district.

- **Yellamma Jatra**: The Yellamma Jatra attracts lakhs of people and is the star attraction of this place. The deity is invited to preside over the function, with mud pots filled with water and chanted Margosa stems. Special prayers are offered by ladies, who are almost naked without outfit, but covering their bodies with knee garlands. They march to the temple in procession to the accompaniment of instrumental music. It is a unique tradition, practiced nowhere.

- **Tirupati Tirumala Brahmotsav:** This festival coincides with Rayalaseema Food and Dance Festival. It is a famous nine days festival celebrated at the world famous Tirumala Venkateswara Temple in Tirupati marked by a beautiful procession of Lord Venkateswara. During the festival, the Utsava – murti (processional deity) of the presiding deity Lord Venkateswara, along with his consorts Sridevi and Bhudevi, is taken on a procession on different Vahanams on the streets (Madaveedulu) surrounding the temple. The celebration attracts pilgrims and tourists from all parts of India and across the world.

- **Pushkaram** is held once in twelve years on the banks of the rivers Godavari, Krishna and Pennar in Andhra Pradesh. The Hindus consider a holy dip in these rivers sacred and so people gather in large numbers on the banks of these rivers sacred and so people gather in large numbers on the banks of these rivers, when the Pushkaram is held. Even before sunrise people take the sacred bath and offer prayers to the Lord. Various rituals are performed and it is believed that a holy dip will wash away all their sins. Cultural programs are organised. Many shops come up in the nearby area selling jewellery, sweets, decorative items etc.

- **Visakha Utsav**: Promote the culture, arts, crafts, music and dance of Visakhapatnam and Andhra Pradesh, this festival is organized by the Andhra Pradesh Tourism Development Corporation. This four day long festival is marked by cultural shows, garment exhibitions, heritage tours, sports events, traditional crafts and flower shows.
- **Bhogi:** Bhogi falls on the 13th / 14th January every year. The day before Makara Sankranti is celebrated as Bhogi. It is a festival of family gathering that brings joy and happiness in the families. The married daughters of the family visit their parents' house along with their husbands and children. The festival is very special for 'kotha allullu' i.e new sons – in – law. It is compulsory for the newlywed daughters to visit their parents' house along with their husband. This biggest festival of Andhra Pradesh involves lots of preparation well in advance which includes clutter – clearing, whitewashing / painting the house, decorating the house and compulsory purchase of clothes for the all the members of the family including the servants of the house.

The Chowki Dinner:

A unique and traditional feature of this cuisine is the famous Chowki dinner.

> *"The Chowki dinner dates back to the Nizam rule in Andhra Pradesh. It was the formal royal dinner of the state then. The dining place or the Shahi Dastarkhwan was a very revered part of the palace then and there is no better way to feel and experience royalty than to eat exactly like them."*

Instead of a dining table, a low table was used to serve and eat food. This table was called *Chowki*. Modern day Chowki dinners use these low tables, cotton mattresses for sitting and bolsters and pillows for comfort. Ideally, in a Chowki dinner the meal is served for eight people who can comfortable sit and eat on a low table and a multi course, typically Hyderabadi dinner is served.

Table covered with embroidered cloth topped with banana leaves on which food is served and eaten. Each dish served in this royal meal is prepared with utmost care to maintain the authenticity. The royal recipes which were once a guarded secret are used to make mouthwatering dishes for this meal.

The setting of the Chowki dinner is such that you will feel that you have travelled back in time and are dinning with the Kings and queens of the era. Meat and vegetable curries in thick gravies, sometimes topped with delightful *Lukhmi*, the irresistible *Nahari*, assortment of different the world famous kababs (*Lagaan ke Kabab*, *Seekh*, *Jhammi* and *Shikhampur*) and keemas, different types of delicious breads are served in well- arranged typical Nawabi style. These succulent preparations will win over your heart worth appreciating.

No Indian meal is complete without a sweet dish. At the end of the Chowki dinner, the diners are served traditional sweet dishes which are a treat for your sweet tooth. The *Kheema* and *Kheer* are prepared with festive flair. You can also have *Double ka meetha* which is a pudding made of bread and garnished with cashews. *Dil – E – Firdaus is* a sweet dish made entirely of milk and *Qubani – Ka Meetha* makes use of apricots.

Along with the exotic dinner, the majestic Deccan ambiance accompanied by traditional entertainment like Ghazals, add to the taste and enjoyment.

Nowadays the Chowki dinner is a paradise for all food lovers.

Classical Andhra Recipes:

Chhas ka shorba:

Ingredients –

- Butter milk – ltr.
- Coconut paste – 20 gm
- Turmeric pdr. – ½ tsp
- Mustard seed – ½ tsp
- Curry leaves – 4 nos.
- Coriander leaves – few
- Oil – 2 tbsp

- Salt – to taste
- Peppercorn – 8 nos
- Cumin – ½ tsp
- Garlic – 2 cloves paste paste
- Coriander pdr. – ½ tsp
- Chili pdr. – ½ tsp

Method –

- Boil chopped carrots, red pumpkin, onion, green chillies in one cup of water.
- Cook on medium heat for eight to ten minutes or till the vegetables are soft.
- Cool the cooked vegetables slightly and make a puree in the blender.
- Add roasted cumin powder, salt and one cup of water to the vegetable puree and bring to a boil.
- Reduce heat, add fresh orange juice and simmer for two to three minutes.
- Stir in fresh cream and serve hot garnished with fresh coriander leaves.

Shikhampuri kebab:

Ingredients –

- Mutton mince – 500 gm
- Roasted chana – 150 gm
- Onions – 100 gm
- Salt – tt
- Chili pdr. – 5 gm
- Egg – 1 no
- Ginger – 10 gm
- Garlic – 10 gm
- Mint – few sprig
- Garam masala – 5 gm
- Turmeric – pinch
- Curd – 150 ml
- Oil – 50 ml
- Gr. Coriander – ½ bunch

- Lime – 1 no
- Gr. Chili – 5 gm
- Fat – to fry

Method –

- Slice half the onion and chop finely the remaining.
- Grind ginger, garlic to paste, mix together mince mutton, half the sliced onion, chilli pdr, salt, garam masala, turmeric and chopped mint.
- Add 2 tbsp of curd and a little water, cover and cook till the meat is tender and fairly dry.
- Remove from fire and grind. Mix with roasted chana flour and lime and beaten egg, divide into even balls and keep aside.
- Tie the curd in muslin cloth and hang it for 4 hour.
- Mix the solid curd with chopped onion, gr, chilies and chopped mint, coriander leaves and salt, mix well.
- Take each ball and flatten it with the palm and stuff with the curd mixture, cover and form into cutlet shape.
- Heat fat and fry Shikhampuri till golden brown.
- Serve hot garnished with lime and onion rings.

Baghare baigan:

Ingredients –

- Brinjals – 450 gm
- Red chilies – 5 gm
- Coconut – 115 gm
- Garlic – 5 gm
- Til seeds – 5 gm
- Onions – 225 gm
- Tamarind – 75 gm
- Jaggary – 5 gm
- Mustard seed – 3 gm
- Turmeric – pinch
- Curry patta – few
- Til oil – 30 ml

- Salt – tt
- Gr. Chilies – 5 gm
- Fat – 50 gm
- Coriander seed – 5 gm

Method –

- Wash the brinjals and cut lengthwise into small pieces.
- Heat oil, fry the brinjals till the skin becomes brown, remove and keep aside. In the same oil fry coriander seeds, red chilies and onions.
- Grind the spices with coconut and garlic.
- Roast til seeds and powder.
- Soak the tamarind in warm water and extract the pulp.
- Add to the ground spices.
- To the remaining oil add chopped green chilies and turmeric and fry well.
- Add brinjals, til powder and jaggary.
- Cover and cook till the gravy thickens and remove from fire.
- Heat fat, add mustard seeds and curry leaves, when they crackle pour over the curry and serve hot.

Hyderabadi Biryani:

Ingredients –

- Mutton – 1 kg
- Semi cooked rice – 750 gm
- Sautéedbrownonions – 100 gm
- Ginger garlic paste – 1 tbsp
- Red chilli paste – 1 tbsp
- Green chilli paste – 1 tbsp
- Cardamom powder – ½ tbsp
- Cinnamon sticks – 3 – 4 nos
- Jeera seeds – 1 tbsp
- Cloves – 4 no
- Lemon juice – 2 tbsp
- Curd – 250 gm

- Clarified butter – 4 tbsp
- Mace – pinch
- Mint leaves chopped – – 1 tbsp
- Saffron – 1 tsp
- Water – cup
- Salt – 1 tbsp
- Oil – 20 ml

Method –

- Mix the mince in ½ cup of water to separate all the pieces.
- Heat oil and add the jeera seeds.
- When the seeds splutter, add the garlic, ginger, onions, bay leaves and the whole garam masala, and stir – fry, till the fat separates.
- Add beaten curd and fry again for 2 minutes.
- Add the tomatoes and continue to stir – fry till the fat separates once again, then add the salt, coriander, haldi, red chilli and black pepper powder.
- Over high heat, add the mince, stir a few times till the colour changes, and then lower the heat.
- Continue to stir fry, till the keema is almost cooked through.
- Add the methi leaves and cook till fat separates once again.
- Serve hot.

Shir sewain:

Ingredients –

- Vermicelli (Sewain) – 250 gm
- Milk – 750 ml
- Sugar – 400 gm
- Ghee – 4 tbsp
- Khoya – 100 gm
- Raisins – 2 tbsp
- Pista nuts – 1 tbsp
- Roasted ,sliced almond – 1 tbsp
- Cashew nuts – 2 tbsp

- Saffron – 1 gm
- Silver leaf – to garnish

Method –

- Soak the saffron strands in1 tbsp of water.
- Fry vermicelli in hot ghee until golden colored. Pour in milk and allow it to simmer for two minutes.
- Add sugar and continue cooking until sugar dissolves.
- Stir in grated khoya, half the raisins and nuts.
- Sprinkle dissolved saffron strands and allover the kheer.
- Decorate with the rest of the nuts and silver leaf
- Serve cold

(Better is eaten after 12 hours of preparation)

CHAPTER FOUR

Tamil Cuisine

Introduction to Tamil Nadu

Tamil Nadu has always been a hub for food connoisseurs to take a great pleasure of some of the finest traditional cuisine in the country. The state is reckoned to be one of the best places in India for offering a bagful of culinary treasure for tourists to savour. But, the fascinating things about Tamil Nadu are the touch of their customary culture which is served with its every delectable fare.

> *"Idli, Sambar, Dosa, Uttapam, and Vada are just a few names whenever it comes to popular South Indian food. Whereas, there are some other equally popular traditional foods of Tamil Nadu that are not much in outside world except the region but are sure to delight your taste buds. The region is known to offer a wide variety of both vegetarian and non – vegetarian dishes with each holding a unique flavor some taste."*

Tamil Nadu is also recognized for its varied range of spices which are also exported in different nations like Chillies, Tamarind, Cardamom, Coriander, Pepper, Curry Leaves, Cloves, and Mint. The state also bids an extensive range of tea, coffee, banana and coconut, which together with other fares, makes Tamil Nadu one of the best food getaways in India. Whereas, the food habit remains almost the same in all season as the weather of the state does not fluctuate much.

The popular cuisine of Tamil Nadu perfectly connects with its people and is incredibly dipped with the right amount and quantity of spices along with all other ingredients.

Geography

Tamil Nadu, located in south India, is bounded on the north by Andhra Pradesh and Karnataka, on the south by the Indian Ocean, on the east by the Bay of Bengal, and by Kerala on the west. The waters of the Bay of Bengal and the Indian Ocean surround the coastal eastern and southern boundaries of the state.

The northern extreme of Tamil Nadu is Pulicat Lake while the southernmost tip is Cape Comorin or Kanyakumari. The Eastern and Western Ghats meet in Tamil Nadu and run along the state's eastern and western borders.

Hill stations like Udhagamandalam (Ooty), Kodaikanal, Kothagiri and Yercaud are situated in this hilly region. It is interesting to note that there are only two major gaps (Palakkad gap and Shencottah gap) into the long chain of hills that border western Tamil Nadu. In a marked contrast to the low rocky hills of the Eastern Ghats, the hills of the Western Ghats have dense forests. The land can be divided into five major physical divisions – the Kurinji or mountainous region, the Mullai or forest region, the Palai or arid region, the Marudham or the fertile plains and the Neidhal or coastal region.

The Eastern and Western Ghats meet in Tamil Nadu and run along its eastern and western boundaries. The Cauvery River, originating in the Coorg district of the neighboring state of Karnataka, is the lifeline of the state. The lush Coromandal plains are irrigated by the Cauvery and its Thanjavur – Nagapattinam delta is called the granary of Tamil Nadu. Palar, Pennar, Vaigai, and Tamiraparani are the other rivers of the state.

History

The history of Tamil Nadu is very old and goes back to thousands of years back. It is believed that the Dravidians of Tamil country were once a part of the early Indus Valley settlers and moved south after the advent of the Aryans around 1500 BC. However, the recorded history of human civilization in Tamil Nadu goes back only to the 4th century BC. Tamil Nadu was ruled by three major dynasties – the Cholas in the east, the Pandyas in the central area and Cheras in the west. This was during the Sangam Age –

the classical period of Tamil literature – that continued for some 300 years after the birth of Christ.

The Pallava dynasty was influential particularly in the 7th and 8th centuries, testimonies to which are the monuments at Mamallapuram. In the 13th century, with threats of Muslim invasions from the north, the southern Hindu dynasties combined and the empire of Vijayanagar, which covered all of South India, was firmly established.

However, by the 17th century, due to the disintegration of the Vijayanagar Empire, various small rulers like the Nayaks ruled southern India. By the middle of the 18th century, there were frequent conflicts between the British, French, and Dutch due to their interest in these areas. The British were finally victorious, while small pockets like Pondicherry and Karaikal remained under French control. Under the British rule, most of south India was integrated into the region called the Madras Presidency. The anti – colonial feeling in Tamil Nadu started as early as 1806 at Vellore.

After independence in 1947, the Madras Presidency became Madras State, comprising of present day Tamil Nadu, coastal Andhra Pradesh, Northern Kerala, and the southwest coast of Karnataka. The state was later divided on linguistic lines. In 1968 the state of Madras was renamed Tamil Nadu.

Culture & Tradition

Tamil Nadu is one of the most urbanized states of India but most of the people still live in villages. The history of the origin of the Tamilians according to the records is said to be more than 2,000 years and they belong to the Dravidian family, an ethnic group from South Asia. They speak the Dravidian language – Tamil. It was believed that they have been living in the southern parts of India and the northeastern parts of Sri Lanka.

In Tamil Nadu, there is an established caste system with traditional differentiations a lot more pronounced than in many other parts of India. When it comes to the ethinicity of the Tamil people, it is usually identified by their jati title or jati name which most of the time defines their language, occupation and political affiliation. About 80 percent of the people in Tamil Nadu follow Hinduism. A substantial percentage of population in Tamil Nadu follows Christianity and Islam.

One of the most ancient and rich traditions in the world is that of the Tamilians. The traditions are part their life and they also strictly adhere to it, which includes lot of rituals and ceremonies and is also a part of their identity across the world. These rich traditions of the Tamil which are deep rooted are supposed to be quite old and have evolved over many centuries.

The tradition of (*rangoli* or the *kolam*) drawing figures at the doorstep is supposed to be a unique culture followed by the Tamils. *Chaula* or *Choodakarana* ceremony, where the hair of one year old child is shaved is still practiced. Hinduism forms the major religion followed in the state followed by Islam, Christianity and Jainism. Their rituals include deity worship and animisms like tree worship, animal worship and stars and planets worship.

Lord Muruga is the chief deity of Tamils and its six abodes are pilgrims centers located in different parts of the state. They are very adherent towards their rituals and traditions like following the caste system, religion and community traits, etc.

Climate

The geographical location of Tamil Nadu is such that the climatic condition shows only slight seasonal variations. Due to close proximity to the Sea, the temperatures and humidity remain relatively high all the year round. The climate of Tamil Nadu is tropical in nature with little variation in summer and winter temperatures. While April – June is the hottest summer period (with the temperature rising up to the 40°C), November – February is the coolest winter period (with temperatures hovering around 20°C), making the climate quite pleasant.

Tamil Nadu gets most of its rains from the North – east Monsoons between October and December while the state remains largely dry during the South West Monsoon season. The average annual rainfall in Tamil Nadu ranges between 25 and 75 inches a year. The mountainous and hilly areas, especially in the extreme western part of the state, receive the most precipitation, while the lower – lying southern and southeastern regions receive the least rainfall. During summers (April to June), the coastal areas of Tamil Nadu become awkwardly warm and humid, but the nights become cool and pleasant due to sea breeze in the afternoon.

During the hot season, the charming hill stations of Tamil Nadu provide much needed respite from heat and humidity. The period between October to March (when the climate becomes pleasantly cool) is the ideal time to visit Tamil Nadu.

Staple Food

Agriculture is the primary occupation of about seventy percent of the rural population of Tamil Nadu which is heavily dependent on the river water and monsoon rains.

The perennial rivers are Palar, Cheyyar, Ponnaiyar, Kaveri, Meyar, Bhavani, Amaravathi, Vaigai, Chittar and Tamaraparani. Non – perennial rivers include the Vellar, Noyyal, Suruli, Siruvani, Gundar, Vaipar, Valparai and Varshali.

"The main food crops that are grown in Tamil Nadu are rice, pulses and oil seeds while the important commercial crops of the state include sugarcane, sunflower, chillies, ginger, gingelly, groundnut, rubber, cotton, cashew and coconut."

Apart from this the other principal crops grown here include Mandarin orange, guava, mango, banana and turmeric, tea, coffee, tamarind and cardamom. This state is the highest producer of bananas and coconuts in the whole country.

It is India's 4th largest producer of rice behind West Bengal, Uttar Pradesh and Punjab. Tamil Nadu has a 1000 km long coastline with equatorial climate, permitting year round fishery and farming. Fishing is also an important economic activity in Tamil Nadu. Opportunities in shrimp farming and processing, crab culture, Seaweed culture, etc. are on the upswing in the state.

Rice is the major staple food of most of the Tamil people. Normally lunch or dinner is a meal of steamed rice (*choru*) served with accompanying items, which typically include sambar, poriyal (curry), any meat or fish, rasam, kootu and curd.

Features of the Tamil Cuisine

Tamil cuisine is characterized by the use of rice, legumes and lentils, its distinct aroma and flavour achieved by the blending of spices including curry leaves, tamarind, coriander, ginger, garlic, chilli, pepper, cinnamon, cloves, cardamom, cumin, nutmeg, coconut and rosewater.

Regional cuisine:

Over a period of time, each geographical area where Tamils have lived has developed its own distinct variant of the common dishes in addition to dishes native to itself. The four divisions of ancient *Tamilakam* are the primary means of dividing Tamil cuisine.

The ***Chettinad region comprising Karaikudi and adjoining areas*** is known for its spicyness of both traditional vegetarian dishes like idiyappam, uthappam, paal paniyaram and non – vegetarian dishes made primarily using chicken. Chettinad cuisine has gained popularity in non – Tamil speaking areas as well. Chettinad is located in the Sivaganga district of southern Tamil Nadu. Standard full meal consisting of cooked dal, eggplant (brinjal) curry, drumstick, sambar, ghee for flavouring rice, and sweetmeats like payasam and paal paniyaram. Chettinad cuisine is one of the spiciest, oiliest and most aromatic cuisines in India. The dishes are hot and pungent with fresh ground masalas.

Madurai, Tirunelveli and the other southern districts of Tamil Nadu are known for non – vegetarian food made of mutton, chicken and fish. Paratha made with maida or all – purpose flour, and loosely similar to the north Indian wheat flour – based Paratha, is served at food outlets in Tamil Nadu, especially in districts like Madurai, Virudhunagar, Tuticorin, Tirunelveli and the adjoining areas. Madurai has its own unique foods such as jigarthanda, muttaiparotta (minced parotta and scrambled egg), paruthipal (made of cottonseeds),Karidosai (dosai with mutton stuffing) & ennaidosai (dosai with lots of oil) which are rarely found in other parts of Tamil Nadu.

Nanjilnadu (Kanyakumari district) region is famous for its fish curry since the region is surrounded by the three great water bodies of Asia: (Indian ocean, Arabian Sea and Bay of Bengal). Fish forms an integral part of life. Owing to its unique cultural affinity and the availability of coconut, coconut oil forms a base for almost all the preparations of the region.

The western Kongunadu region has specialities like Santhakai/Sandhavai (a noodle like item of rice), Oputtu (a sweet tasting pizza – like dish that is dry outside with a sweet stuffing), and kola urundai (meatballs), Thengai Paal (sweet hot milk made of jaggery, coconut and cotton seeds), Ulundu Kali(Sweet made out of Jaggery, Gingely Oil and Black Gram), Ragi puttumavu, Arisi Puttumavu, Vazhaipoo Poriyal, Kambu Paniyaram, Ragi Pakoda, Thengai Parpi, Kadalai Urundai, Ellu Urundai, Pori Urundai. The natural crops of this region forms the main ingredients in this Kongunadu cuisine.

Ceylon Tamil cuisine, bears similarities to Tamil Nadu cuisine but also has many unique vegetarian and non – vegetarian dishes. It features dishes such as (steamed rice cake) and *idiyappam or sevai*, (known in other parts of the world as string hoppers).

Eating – out in its capital city Chennai, is a great experience and provides a glimpse of the unique lifestyle of the city. Chennai is known for its cuisine, brought to the city by people who have migrated from different parts of Tamil Nadu. Chennai has a large collection of restaurants, some of them are unique 'Speciality Restaurants,' which serve 'Indian Cuisine' with an ambience to match, while most others cater South Indian tiffin and meals, at very reasonable prices.

Features of the cuisine:

- Chettinad cuisine is one of the spiciest, oiliest and most aromatic cuisines in India. The dishes are hot and pungent with fresh ground masalas.
- Oil and spices are liberally used in cooking and most dishes have generous amounts of peppercorn, cinnamon, bay leaves, cardamom, fenugreek, saunf, nutmeg, green and red chillies, marathi mokku, anasipoo, kalpasi, patthar ke phool etc. Tamarind is also used in this cuisine.
- *Coconut oil* is used as the medium of cooking. Gingelly oil or sesame seed oil is used for finishing some dishes.
- *Rice* is the staple food of Tamil Nadu. *Parboiled rice* is eaten for its high nutritive value and this dominates in all the dishes starting from appetizers to desserts. They eat Rice (staple diet) with sambar, dhal, kootu, vegetable curry, papad, buttermilk. Black rice (*Kavunarisi*) is used commonly in Chettinad cuisine to prepare sweet puddings.
- *Arhar dal, urad dal and chana dal* are the commonly used lentils.
- Rice is usually combined with the lentils to make various dishes like idlis, dosas, vadas, uttapams. These are usually *fermented* for easy digestion as well as development of the typical sour flavour.
- *Coconut, tamarind and asafoetida* are a must for almost all vegetarian recipes.

- Tamil people use a variety of ingredients like ginger, garlic, pepper, nutmeg, tamarind, chilly, cumin, cardamom, coconut, *Marathi mokku* (capers), Stone flower (*kalpasi*), Fresh neem flower (*Veepam poo*) and curry leaves to give aroma and superb taste to their foods.
- Food is generally more towards the *spicy* (due to the use of crushed black pepper corn, red and green chillies) and *sour* side (which is due to fermentation and also due to the extensive use of tamarind).
- Curd also finds a common use in the cuisine and is utilised to balance the hotness which results due to the use of spices.
- *Coconut chutney and sambar* invariably form a part of most of the Tamil dishes. *Mulaga podi* (a powdered mix of several dried lentils with oil or ghee) is also serves at times.
- Use of various *seafoods and chicken* is also common.
- A major feature of Tamil Nadu cuisine is the wide varieties of *Tiffin items*. They are served in the evening as a snack and a few tiffin items also feature in the breakfast. *Dishes like idli, sevai, upma, pongal,, uttapam, dosai, puttu, aval, chapathi, adai, Vadai.*
- Filter coffee is the main beverage along with this tiffin.
- The Chettinad people through their mercantile contacts with Burma, learnt to prepare a type of rice pudding made with sticky red rice. Kavunarisi – a black rice is also used to prepare desserts.

Tamil feast – Virundhu Sappadu:

- During a **Virundhu Sappadu**, the feastly meal, the guests sits on a mat and the meal is served on a banana leaf which is spread in front of the guests. Traditionally, the banana leaf is laid so that the leaf tip is pointed left.
- The dishes are served in a particular order, and each dish has its own specific spot on the leaf. Everyone starts together and ends the meal together.
- The top half of the banana leaf is for the side dishes and the bottom part is for the main dish. Payasam, Kesari, Sweet Pongal or any Dessert also occupies a portion of the bottom part. The top left includes a pinch

of salt, a dash of pickle and a spoon of salad, a spoon of pachadi. In the middle of the leaf there may be a banana chips, potato chips and fried papads and a vadai. The top right hand corner is reserved for spicy foods including a wide array of curries and gravies. Dry and wet curries are placed one after the other. They are called poriyal and koothu. A minimum of three curries are served in a feast.

-
- Traditionally, sweets are eaten first. Sambar rice is eaten first with a spoon of ghee. This is followed by Kuzhambu and then Rasam. Finally rice with curd or buttermilk is eaten at the end of the meal. In the end, the meal is complete with a banana.
- The style of service and the items offered in *Virundhu Sappadu* has got regional variations too.

Tamil meal design:

- *Breakfast or tiffin*includes *idli* (steamed rice cakes), *dosai* (a pancake made from a batter of rice and lentils crisp fried on a pan), *vada* (deep fried doughnuts made from a batter of lentils), *pongal* (a mash of rice and lentils boiled together and seasoned with ghee, cashew nuts, pepper and cumin seed), *uppuma* (cooked semolina seasoned in oil with mustard, pepper, cumin seed and dry lentils.)
- There are several variations of the dishes mentioned above which are eaten with *coconut chutney, sambar* (seasoned lentil broth) and *mulaga podi* (a powdered mix of several dried lentils eaten with oil).
- *Lunch* or *meals* consists of cooked rice served with an array of vegetable dishes, sambar, chutneys, rasam (a hot broth made with tamarind juice and pepper) and curd (yogurt – *Moru/Thayir*). For a non – vegetarian lunch, curries or dishes cooked with mutton, chicken or fish is included. The meals are incomplete without crisp papads or appalam. After finishing their meal, they like to have payasam.
- *For **dinner**,* Tamilians eat uthappam, dosa, idli or simply rice kanji (gruel). They also have milk before going to bed.

Filter coffee of Tamil Nadu:

The making of the famous filter coffee is traditional, where coffee beans are first roasted and then ground. The powder is then added into a filter and boiling hot water is added to it, to prepare the decoction. The decoction is then added to milk with sugar. The drink is poured from one container to another in rapid succession to make an ideal frothy cup of filter coffee. It is also known as *meter kapee* as it is poured from a small steel glass into a bowl (katori) and vice varsa from almost a distance of a meter to make it frothy.

Common Equipments and Utensils:

- *Eyya Chombu:* It is a vessel made from tin to impart the right flavour to rasam
- *Kal Chatti:* It is a stoneware used for preparing tempering
- *Kuziappa Chatti:* It is normally made of heavy bronze. It is circular in shape and has shallow depressions resembling a cup. The leftover sour dosa batter is poured inside it and cooked.
- *Thenkuzal Naazhi:* This equipment is used for making crisp lentil fritters called murukkus. It can also be used to press the rice dough to make vermicelli.
- *Dosa Thiruppi:* A flat slicer that is used for spreading oil on the dosa and also for scraping dosa off the hot plate or tawa.
- *Addaikal:* it is a thicker tawa than the dosa tawa usually used for cooking addai and hence the name.
- *Idli Panai:* This vessel is used for making idlis, as many as 40 – 50 idlis can be made together depending on the number of plated used.
- *Thuruvammai:* It is an equipment, used both as a coconut scraper and as a vegetable chopper. This is used in some households to cut fish or meat.
- *Uruli:* It is very heavy pot that is used for cooking. Sambhar, vegetables and meat are using are usually cooked using the vessel. They come in a range of sizes depending on the quantity of food to be cooked. This is a very beneficial vessel because the food cooked in this vessel remains hot for a long time.

Speciality Tamil Dishes:

Chicken Chettinad: A popular chicken curry, cooked in a peppery authentic Chettinad paste laced with coconut and onions. Bring some magic to your plate with this southern style chicken dish.

Coconut chutney: Uruttu Chammanti is the local name for coconut chutney in Tamil Nadu. It is made with grounded coconut, dry red chilly (particularly roasted red chilly) ginger, mustard seed and served cold along with the dishes such as Dosa, Idli, Vada.

Dosa / dosai: These are made from rice and urad dal and the batter is fermented. This fermented batter is cooked on a large tawa in shape of pancakes. They are filled with various types of fillings.

Idli: Idlis made in South India are of various kinds and each has its own traditional ways. The process of cooking is however common for all which is steaming. The most common one is made with urad dal and parboiled rice. The batter is made by grinding both separately and leaving it overnight to ferment. The next day it is steamed in the idli vessel.

Kolambhu: Kolambhu or kozhambu is a thin stew of vegetables with spices. It can also be of various types. The most common type is moar kolambhu, where buttermilk is used as the base and thickened with a paste of rice and lentils to make it into a spicy stew with vegetables inside.

Koottu: There are many varieties of koottu. It is usually made by boiling green gram along with bite size pieces of vegetables and also fruits such as jackfruit and raw bananas. It is flavoured with turmeric and red chillies. Grated coconut and rice paste are used for thickening the koottu. It is usually finished with coconut oil.

Kootu: Kootu is a semi – solid side dish that's made of lentils and vegetables. It is most commonly served with Virundhu Sappadu that's a combo of boiled rice, curd, rasam, poriyal and pickle. There are many variations of Kootu that are prepared in Tamil Nadu. Poricha kootu or fried kootu which is made of Urad dhal and pepper fried in red chillies, cumin and fresh coconut made into a paste. Vegetables and moong dal are cooked separately following which they are heated and mixed with the paste. Snake guard and beans are the common ingredients in this kootu.

Koozh: Koozh is the Tamil name of Millet Porridge that's commonly sold by street vendors. It is made from Cumbu flour or broken rice in a clay pot. Although it is a vegetarian recipe, Koozh is also made of fish, chicken and crab.

Kozhambu: It is a gravy preparation with a base of tamarind, whole red chillies, toor dal and urad dal.

Kuzhi Paniyaram: Paniyaram is a South Indian dish that's made of steaming batter using a mould with cavities. The batter is made of rice and black lentils, similar to the one used for idly and dosa. People have experimented with the dish in many ways, it can be made spicy, savoury, sweet depending on your likes. Only ingredients like jaggery, chillies, masala vary.

LemonRice: A seasoning of onions, tomatoes, curry leaf, red chilly, salt and lemon juice is made and cooked rice is added and fried with the seasoning. Some groundnuts and added to the dish to give it some crunchiness and balance out the sour taste of lemon and served with chutney or vegetable salad.

Manjal Milagu Paal: Also called as the turmeric – pepper milk, this is one the traditional drinks of Tamil Nadu. People drink it every day before going to bed. It also acts as a medicine and prevents the body from flu as well as a cough and cold.

Mulligataw ny Soup: It is an International soup from tamil Nadu. This recipe has a host of chillies and spices, along with potato, apples and carrots, cooked with spices and lentils, blended into puree and finished with coconut milk.

Muruku: Muruku is one of the most famous snacks that got its origin from Tamil Nadu, and its name means twisted. Again, the batter for the muruku is made by a mixture of rice flour and urad dal with some salt, water, cumin seed etc. It is then deep fried in oil in various shapes till it turns hard.

NaralchiVadi: Also known as Coconut Barfi, it is made of coconut powder or grated coconut, condensed milk and sugar. It is a very famous dessert.

Nei Payasum: Made of rice, jaggery, ghee, cashew nuts and raisins, this dish is a well – liked dessert item. It is specially made for occasions like birthdays or even when people visit each other houses. Tamil people have a ritual of serving it as a dessert before the meal.

Pachadi: These can be regarded as South Indian raitas. A variety of ingredients such as grated carrots, deep fried sliced okra, roasted and mashed brinjals etc are mixed along with smooth thick curd to prepare pachadi. These are served tempered with curry leaves, mustard, urad dal, and whole red chillies. The ingredient used with the curd can be sauted or deep fat fried before being added to it.

Paruppu Payasam: It is made by roasting Moong dal and cooking it soft. Some jaggery syrup is added to the mashed moong dal and stirred till completely cooked. This is then served with roasted cashew nuts and tastes very rich and creamy.

Payasam: It is a sweet preparation made withn rice, jaggery and coconut milk.

Pongal: This is a staple meal during every auspicious festival of Tamil Nadu. Besides the rice and sweet milk, the dish is cooked with ingredients like cardamom, green gram, raisins and cashew nuts. According to the traditional beliefs, Pongal is cooked in open space in the sunlight, as it is dedicated to the sun god.

Poriyal: Poriyal is a bit sauteed vegetable dish that's made of shredded or diced vegetables fried in spices. The recipe is a fusion of frying mustard seeds, onions and urad dal with the vegetable of your choice in turmeric, dried red chillies, spices and coriander. In certain places, shredded coconut is used to dress the dish.

Puliodarai/Pullihara: "Kokum Rice" or "Tamarind Rice" is a common rice preparation in the South Indian states of Tamil Nadu. It is prepared with Kokum or tamarind and jaggery cooked in oil and mixed with rice along with spices and curry leaves.

Sambar: Sambar is a curry just like the dal but what make it differ is the different spices and vegetables that are used to prepare it. Sambar is a little sour because of the tamarind base that it is prepared in, and consists of various vegetables. Some of the famous vegetables used to make Sambar are: Drumsticks, Brinjal, Pumpkin, potatoes and radish. One of the main ingredients that gives it the taste is the use of curry leaves. This Tamil Nadu food accompaniment is served with almost all the South Indian dishes be it rice, idli, dosa etc

Sundal: It is the easiest evening snack that can be prepared within a short time. It is made of soaked beans along with onion, chilies, and grated coconut. It is made into a salad and is usually served in the evening. It is a very healthy dish and also serves the purpose of an evening snack.

Takkali Sadam: Also called tomato rice, it is made of rice, onions, tomatoes and other ingredients. It is made in the form of a pulav and the main ingredient used is tomato which gives it a tangy taste. It is bit little spicy. This dish is the most common type of rice after plain white rice which is served during lunch.

Ven Pongal: It is an authentic breakfast item of Tamil Nadu. It is made of boiled rice and yellow daal and tempered with pepper, cumin seeds, and ghee. Served hot, it gives out a mouth – watering smell and forms a perfect breakfast item.

Tamil Nadu Festivals:

- *Pongal:* This is the most important Harvest festival celebrated by the people of Tamil Nadu. It lasts for a period of 4 days and is normally celebrated on the 13 to 16 January (*Margali* month). This festival is actually mainly celebrated to thank or show appreciation to the Sun God for giving energy towards good agriculture of crops like rice, sugarcane, turmeric etc (an essential ingredient in Tamil cooking). The term *'Pongal'* in Tamil means "to boil", and this festival is celebrated as a thanksgiving ceremony for the year's harvest. The people boil the first rice of the season as a tribute to the Sun God. Pongal is also the name of a dish that is sweetened rice boiled with lentils. It is a very famous in the South and is cooked for most of the festivals there.
- *Puthandu:* Also called the Tamil New Year which falls in mid of April. The morning of Puthandu is marked as Women make beautiful *Kolams* (colourful designs at the entrance of the house) at the entrance of their houses. Trees laden with mangoes and bloomed neem marks the prosperity of the people. On this day people wear new clothes and eat delicious food one of them being „*Maanga Pachadi"* a sweet and sour dish made with mangoes, Jaggery and Neem flowers.
- *Thaipusam:* Thaipusam is a Hindu festival celebrated mostly by the Tamil community. The colorful celebration is one of the important fairs and festivals in not just India but also countries like Malaysia, USA, Sri Lanka, Thailand and other countries where Tamil Community has major presence. Thaipusam is celebrated each year on the full moon in the month of January/February. It's a time to ask Lord Murugan, son of Lord Shiva, for forgiveness, good health and peace in the New Year. Devotees carry the *kavadis* to ask for forgiveness, keep a vow or offer thanks to Lord Subramaniam (son of Lord Siva). As part of the festival's rituals, many participants engage in various acts of devotion and control over their senses including piercing the skin, tongue or cheeks. Some walk over burning coals.

- *Mahamaham Festival:* This is a Hindu Festival that is celebrated once in 12 years in the State in a small town called *Kumbakonam*. It is a bathing ceremony that is believed to cleanse one of their sins and is attended by thousands of Hindu devotees who take a dip in *Mahamaham tank*.

- *Shivarathri:* This holy festival is celebrated in all Shiva temples of the country usually in February or March. Special poojas and chanting is performed to remark this auspicious day. Devotees observe fasting and remain awake throughout the night. Anointing and purification of Lingams begins from midnight.

- *Vaikunta Ekadasi:* In order to celebrate the opening of the gates of heaven, Vaikunta Ekadasi is commemorated in late December. All Vishnu temples get a decorative erected known as „*Vaikuntha Vasal*". Hundreds of people enter the gate and offer special prayers and Bhajans. Many stay awake throughout the night and break their fast by feasting early in the morning.

- *Aadi Perukku:* Aadi Perukku is the eighteenth day of the Tamil month Adi, (mid July to mid – August). The rivers are immensely flooded with water and over flow. People celebrate this day by preparing sweet treats and traditional delicacies. People offer prayers and float their offerings on the river.

- *Velankanni Festival:* The renowned and revered church of Velankanni near Nagapattinam has divine legends. This church has a wondrous image of *Our Lady of Velankanni*. Portuguese sailors had suffered from a shipwreck and had built this shrine as a thanksgiving. They wanted to thank Our Lady of guiding them safely to shore. Our Lady of Velankanni is known to have miraculous powers which attract thousands of visitors every year during September and October.

- *Kanthuri Festival:* This festival is devoted to celebrate saint *Quadirwali*. This festival has a secular nature. On this auspicious day, one of the descendants is declared as a successor or 'peer'. This peer is then offered gifts. The tomb of the saint is anointed with sandal paste which is later distributed to all devotees. This holy sandal paste is believed to possess special powers and acts as a remedy for illness. Kanthuri Festival is celebrated at Nagore durgah near Nagapattinam.

- *Jallikattu Bull Festival:* This festival is celebrated in the month of January on the third day of Pongal festival in Tiruchirapalli, Jallikattu is a bull taming traditional sport played in villages of Tamilnadu. The sport is played in an open ground where a bull is let loose amid hordes of people who try to control the bull by piling on its hump or horns. Tamils consider Jallikattu as a symbol of dignity of its outstanding culture and hence is engraved in the pages of Tamil history.

- *Chitthirai Festival:* Chitthirai festival is the cardinal festival celebrated for 10 days in all temples across Tamil Nadu in April. This festival is also known as *Brahmothsavam.* Every deity is carried for procession every day on different carriages sculpted in the forms of bull, horse, lion, swan, moon and sun. Millions of people visit Tamil Nadu to participate in this festival. Major attractions is the procession of lord kallazhagar otherwise known as lord Vishnu from Azhagarkoil to give away his sister goddess Meenakshi, in Marriage to Lord Sundareswarar.

- *Saral Vizha:* Saaral Vizha is a novel festival celebrated in the month of August to commemorate waterfalls in the region of Kuttalam. Thousands of visitors bathe under waterfalls believing the water has special magical powers. The water rejuvenates the body and refreshes the mind.

Chettinad Cookery:

Chettinad Cuisine is the cuisine of the Chettinad region of Tamil Nadu. Food from this state is predominantly vegetarian due the majority of Tamil Brahmins. The Chettinad region comprises of 76 villages and 2 towns and is dominated by the Chettiar community. Cuisine of Chettinad is uses a variety of freshly ground spices including cumin, fenugreek, fennel, clove, bay leaf, turmeric and tamarind. The cuisine is well known for the complexity of flavours.

The traditional Chettinad cuisine is well known for using so many varieties of spices like star anise, whole red chillies, fennel seed, cinnamon, cloves, bay leaf, peppercorn, cumin seeds and fenugreek. In Chettinad cuisine, common "secret" ingredients are dried flower pods, and kalpasi **(black stone flower)**. The richness of the gravies is increased by addition of tomatoes, coconut, ginger and garlic. Traditionally, the spices were grounded using grinding stones. Chettinad cuisine is loaded with distinct aromas and flavours.

Another distinct feature of this cuisine is that it uses **sun-dried vegetables** and meats in the dishes, which helps in preserving their nutritional value. Most curries and gravies are served with rice-based preparations like Appams, Idlis, Idiyappams, Adais and Dosais because the mild taste of these accompaniments compliments the spiciness of the dishes. Their meals are also accompanied by buttermilk to bring down the heat of the curries served with the dishes.

This community lives in proximity of sea, which makes fish curry, crab masala and prawn masala as their popular dishes. When the community later settled near the coastline, they included some other animal foods like jungle fowl, kada (quail), muyal (rabbit), and pitta (turkey) in their signature dish list. Most of these are eaten with rice and other rice based food accompaniments such as dosas, uppams, idiyappams, and idlis.

Talking of Cheetinad cuisine, they offer both vegetarian and non-vegetarian dishes. Some of the popular dishes include 'Idiyappam', 'Paal Payasam', 'Chicken Chettinad', 'Palkatti Chettinadu', 'Paniyaram', 'Urlai Roast', 'Vellai Paniyaram', 'Kozhakattai', 'Aatukkari Kuzhambu with Steamed Rice', 'Nariyal and Soya Paneer Vada' 'Kozhambu', 'Cabbage Poriyal' 'Karuppatti Paniyaram', 'Kuzhi Paniyaram', 'Vellai Kurma', 'Kaikari Pirattal' and many more.

Traditionally, meals served in Chettinad cuisine are on banana leaves with servings of rice, buttermilk, pickles, papads and salads. They follow a specific protocol where each dish served should be at a designated space and order on the banana leaf. Chettiars are superstitious in nature, so they prefer to serve their dishes in odd numbers of seven or nine.

Chicken Chettinad:

A fiery curry, Chicken Chettinad is one of the most popular dishes that hails from the South Indian region. This delicious curry is prepared with freshly ground coconut along with a number of spices, all of these together make this dish a treat for your senses. Serve it with rice or rotis for a hearty meal.

Recipe of Chicken Chettinad:
Ingredients –

- Chicken 500 grams (with grams)
- Ginger 1 tbsp chopped finely
- Garlic 1 tbsp chopped finely
- Cinnamon 1"
- Cardamom 3
- Cloves 5
- Curry leaf 1 bunch

- Onions 3 chopped finely
- Tomatoes 4 boiled, skinned and chopped
- Red chili powder 1 tsp
- Grated coconut 1.5 cups
- Turmeric 1/2 Tsp
- Poppy seeds 2 tsp
- Coriander seeds 1 tbsp
- Fennel seeds 1 tbsp
- Cumin Seeds 1 tsp
- Dried red chillies 4-5
- Peppercorns 6-8
- 2 teaspoons lemon juice
- Oil 7-8 tbsp
- Salt to taste

Method -

- In a bowl, add salt, turmeric powder and lemon juice with chicken and mix well. Let it marinate for 15 to 20 mins. This will help in making the chicken soft and reduce the cooking time.
- Take a deep bottom non-stick pan and heat oil over moderate flame. Once the oil is hot start adding cumin seeds, coriander seeds, fennel seeds, whole cloves, cardamoms, whole red chilies, peppercorns, cinnamon and saute for a few seconds.
- Remove the spices from flame and allow to cool. Grind the mixture into a coarse grain powder.
- In another pan, heat the oil and add the curry leaves. When they stop spluttering, add the sliced onions and ginger-garlic paste and fry till the paste turns light brown in color.
- Add the grounded spice paste and star anise and fry for another 2-3 minutes.
- Now, add the tomatoes and marinated chicken and saute for 10-15 minutes. Stir well to mix all the ingredients, so that the spices coat the chicken pieces perfectly.
- Add 1/2 cup of water along with grated coconut and mix well. Cover it with a lid and simmer till it is tender. Keep tossing the chicken and add more water if needed to get the desired consistency. When the chicken is done add 2 tsp of lime juice, mix well and turn off the flame.

- Garnish with some tempered curry leaves and serve hot with rice, appam or phulka.

Other Classical Tamil Recipes:

Rasam:

Ingredients-

- Arhar dal-50 gm
- Tomatoes-115 gms
- Lime-1 no
- Curry leaves-2 sprigs
- Green coriander-1/2 bunch
- Tempering
- Mustard seed-1tsp
- Black gram-2 gms
- Cumin-pinch
- Red chilies-2 nos
- Hing-pinch
- Oil-10 ml
- Salt- to taste
- Green chilies-5 gm

Method-

- Boil the dal using enough water till tender.
- Cut tomatoes into pieces, slit green chilies and chop green coriander.
- Add the sliced and chopped ingredients into the dal with curry leaves and bring to boil.
- Heat oil n a fry pan and temper all the ingredients.
- When the spices crackle add to the boiling rasam.
- Check seasonings and again boil for 5-10 minutes.
- Removed from heat, add limejuice and serve hot.

Mulligatawny Curry:

Ingredients-

- Mutton cut-500gms
- Small onion-115 gm
- Ginger-15 gm
- Garlic-5 gm
- Cinnamon-2 gm
- Tomatoes-225 gm
- Curry leaves-2 sprigs Seasoning and thickening
- Red chilies-5 gm
- Coriander- 15 gms
- Cumin-5 gms
- Fenne-l5 gms
- Peppercorn-4 nos
- Bengal gram dal-15 gm
- Coconut milk-300ml
- Salt - to taste

Method-

- Cook the mutton with the first lot of ingredients adding sufficient water till the meat is tender.
- Roast and grind red chilies.
- Roast Bengal gram dal and grind well.
- Mix all the ingredients with coconut milk and turmeric.
- Add it to the mulligatawny and lastly add the limejuice, remove from fire.

Sambhar:

Ingredients-

- Ladies finger-30 gm
- Brinjal-50 gm
- Drumsticks-120 gm
- Arhar dal-100gm

- Turmeric-a pinch
- Coconut oil-as required
- Salt- to taste
- Tamarind-20 gm

Roast and powder -

- Coriander seeds-20 gm
- Red chilies-5 gm
- Chana dal-3 gm
- Urad dal-3 gm
- Fenugreek-2 tsp
- Grated coconut-30 gm
- Rice-3 gm
- Mustard seed-3 gm
- Cumin-a pinch
- Pepper corn-4 nos

Tempering -

- Red chilies-3 nos
- Curry leaves-few sprigs
- Mustard seeds-2 gms
- Asafetida-1 tsp

Method -

- Boil the dal, add cut vegetables into small even sized pieces and powdered spices and cook till the dal is tender. Add tamarind juice extracted in a cup of hot water. Bring to boil. Adjust seasoning and remove.
- Heat coconut oil in a fry pan, add mustard seed, and curry leaves and red chilies and asafetida (previously soaked in a tbsp. of hot water)
- Pour over the sambhar and serve.

Note: You can use red pumpkin or ghiya also in this recipe.

Lime Rice:

Ingredients-

* Basmati rice-200 gm
* Chana dal-1 tsp
* Curry leaves-10 nos
* Cumin-1 tsp
* Turmeric- 1/2 tsp
* Mustard seeds-1 tsp
* Hing-1/4 tsp
* Gr. Chilies-3 chopped
* Coconut-2 tbsp grated
* Gr. Coriander- 1 sprig
* Lemon juice-2 tbsp
* Oil-30 ml
* Salt- to taste

Method-

* Heat 5 tbsp of oil in a pan. Add the chana dal; curry leaves, cumin seeds, mustard seeds, hing, chilies, turmeric and rice.
* Stir-fry for 5 minutes on low flame. Add salt and 4 cups of hot water and cook the rice till dry and soft.
* Turn out on a rice dish.
* Garnish with chopped gr. coriander leaves, coconut and serve after sprinkling lemon juice.

Pal Paysam:

Ingredients-

* Thick milk- 1 liter.
* Rice- 150 gm
* Sugar- 200 gm
* Sultanas- 20 gm
* Cashew nuts- 20 gm

- Desi ghee- 30 ml
- Water- 200 ml

Method-

- Pick, wash and soak the rice for ½ hour.
- Cook the rice with water and half of the milk till soft.
- Add the rest of the milk and sugar and cook till it becomes thick , mix well.
- Fry nuts and sultanas, add to the payasam.
- Powder cardamom and sprinkle over. Pour clarified butter and serve at room temperature.

Avial: (Tamil)

Ingredients -

- 1 cup Green peas (fresh or frozen),
- 2 nos Carrots (peeled and cut into inch rounds Medium yellow squash),
- 10 nos French Bean, cup 2
- Capsicum, cut into 1 inch strips,
- 10 nos Green beans,
- 1 cup French cut Fresh curry leaves,
- 1 Tbsp Turmeric powder Ground,
- 10 tbsp coconut,
- 5 nos Green chillies, seeded and minced,
- 1 tbsp Cumin seeds,
- 1 cup Plain yoghurt, Salt to taste,
- 1 tsp coconut oil.

Method -

- In a large saucepan combine the peas, carrots, squash, bell peppers, beans, turmeric, and curry leaves.
- Add a cup of water and bring to a boil. Reduce heat and simmer partially covered until vegetables are tender and have absorbed all the liquid (10 minutes).

- Do not let the vegetables get too mushy. The slight crunch of the vegetables adds to the flavour of the dish.
- In a bowl whisk the yoghurt and set aside.
- In a blender mix the coconut, chillies and cumin seeds into a paste using very little water.
- Add this to the yoghurt and mix the salt into this seasoned yoghurt.
- Add to the cooked vegetables in the pan.
- Sprinkle the coconut oil and mix well taking care not to break the vegetables.
- Cover and simmer over very low heat until the mixture is warmed through. Serve hot.

CHAPTER FIVE

Malayali Cuisine

Introduction to Kerala (Malayali) Cuisine

Kerala, lovingly called "God"s own country" is truly a land of eternal bliss and a tropical Eden with the mesmerizing beauty of its sun bathed golden seashores edged with abundant coconut trees, the zigzag rocky terrain of the Western Ghats, straggling plantations and paddy fields, the cerulean lagoons and the bountiful rivers and mighty waterfalls, fascinating bio – diversity of its flora and fauna.

The age – old heritage and tradition, bright festivals and dances, and elating boat races are among Kerala's prime attractions. Kerala is an epicurean paradise and the Keralian cuisine is one of the cuisine that enjoy worldwide recognition and appreciation, which one can describe as extremely exotic and relishing.

Kerala has been influenced by many culinary methods in past which are deeply rooted in the traditional Keralian cuisine in the lives of people. Cooking in Kerala is more than just preparation of food. It is a celebration of the rich culture that is deeply imbued in the life of Keralian.

This south Indian state that cradles between Western Ghats and Arabian Sea swings between juicy seafood and aromatic traditional dishes. It is indeed true that the geography culture and to some extent history play an important role in giving the cuisine of Kerala some unforgettable flavour. Kerala cuisine is famous for its mouthwatering recipes and authentic Malayali dishes.

Kerala food is spicy and delectable. Kerala has its own distinctive cuisine using the ingredients locally available. Sea food is popular among Malayalis. The evolution of the culinary style of Kerala can be traced to the society, culture, history and topography of the state.

Geography

Kerala is the one place with many diverse geographical features. The state is divided into three geographical regions: Highlands, which slope down from the Western Ghats onto the Midlands of undulating hills and valleys into an unbroken 580 km long coastline with many picturesque backwaters, interconnected with canals and rivers. The wild lands are covered with dense forests, while other regions lie under tea and coffee plantations or other forms of cultivation.

Most of the state is engulfed in rich greenery which ensures a very calming experience at all times. The state bears many rivers with innumerable tributaries and distributaries. These rivers are Monsoon – fed and hence, may turn into rivulets in summer. There are 41 west – flowing rivers and three east – flowing rivers which pass across Kerala with their innumerable tributaries and branches. These rivers are Monsoon – fed and hence, may turn into rivulets in summer.

The Kerala Backwaters region is a particularly well – recognized feature of Kerala; it is an interconnected system of brackish water lakes and river estuaries that lies inland from the coast and runs virtually the length of the state. These facilitate inland travel throughout a region roughly bounded by Thiruvananthapuram in the south and Vatakara (which lies some 450 km to the north). There are 34 backwaters in Kerala.

Lake Vembanad—Kerala's largest body of water dominates the backwaters; it lies between Alappuzha and Kochi and is over 200 km² in area.

History

Kerala – God's Own Country lends its name from a very famous old legend. As the legend has it that God Parshuram an incarnation or avatar of Mahavishnu saved Kerala from the raging and belligerent Sea. Since then people believe it to be a land of God. Due to the convenient location, this land established trade contacts with Egypt, Greeks, Assyria, Romans and the Chinese.

The Malayalam era *'Kollavarsha'* is said to have originated in the 9th century A.D. We have recorded evidence of the first chief kingdom that ruled Kerala. It was the ancient Chera Empire whose court language was

Tamil and the founder was Cheraman Perumal.

Kerala was first cited in the Sanskrit epic Aitareya Aranyaka which formed the basis of written records. Later Panini mentioned Kerala in his works. Kerala also lured the Greeks, Christians, Arabs and Muslims, Portuguese, Dutch and other communities of the world with its rich culture and natural resources. Vasco Da Gama's discovery of Calicut and his arrival in 20th May, 1498 made the Portuguese control the money – spinning pepper trade.

In 1868 the ancient sage Agasthya introduced the Vedic Hinduism to Kerala and South India. Finally the Mauryans and the Grand Mughals consolidated their empires in Kerala. In the meantime the Dutch drove away the Portuguese from Kozhikode (Calicut). Then Mysore's Hyder Ali invaded north Kerala and Kozhikode in 1766. In 1792 Tipu Sultan surrendered Kerala to the British.

It was in 1949 that the three territories Travancore, Kochi and Malabar were merged and in 1956 the state of Kerala came into existence and became a part of the Indian Union. Kerala is also justly proud of its reputation for healthcare and education, with literacy rates that stand, officially at least, at 96 percent for men and 92 percent for women.

Climate

The coastal state of Kerala lying on the Southwestern tip of India has commonly been called the tropical paradise of India. Bounded by Arabian Sea at one side and the Western Ghats on the other, the beautiful land with stunning beauty has an equable and tropical climate offering a pleasing atmosphere throughout the entire year. Owing to its diversity in geographical features, the climatic condition in Kerala is diverse. It can be divided into 4 seasons – summer, south – west monsoon, north – east monsoon and winter. In summer (March to June) the state experiences hot, humid and pleasant climate and the temperature reaches to a maximum of 33 degrees centigrade, followed by South West Monsoon that starts pouring in the month of June and continues till August. The month of September to November gets light pours from the North – East Monsoon. Precipitation averages about 115 inches annually statewide, with some slopes receiving more than 200 inches. With the arrival of winter there is certain drop in the temperature (to low as 10^{0}C) and you can feel a slight chill due to the cold wind. Winter in Kerala lasts from November to January or February.

Staple Malayali Foods

With excellent agro – climatic conditions, agriculture is the state's main economic activity. The staple crop grown in Kerala is the rice or paddy and coconut. There are about 600 varieties of rice grown here. Kuttanad in Alleppey district is called —*The rice bowl of Kerala*‖. The crop that is grown in plenty next to rice is tapioca. It is cultivated in the drier regions and is a major food of the Keralites. Pulses (e.g., peas and beans) sorghum, cashewnut, arecanut, and coconut cultivation is also done in quantity in the State. The state also boasts for its best quality and large production of fruits like mangoes, jackfruit, cherries and bananas.

Kerala can be termed as the land of spices, considering the large variety of spices grown in the state. It is the largest producer of pepper in India. 96% of India's national output of pepper is produced from Kerala. Apart from pepper, other spices produced in the state include ginger, cardamom, nutmeg, tamarind, clove, cinnamon, vanilla and turmeric etc.

Commercial poultry farming and fishing is well developed and perhaps the major blooming industry. The state is a national leader in fish production. Sardines, tunas, mackerels, and prawns are among the principal products of the industry. Though fishing is not a source of life for the Keralites but still lots of fresh sea fish are exported to various parts of the country. The farming community involves a lot of animal husbandry. Animals like chicken, ducks, cows, goats, buffaloes and elephants are reared and used in day to day life of the people.

Features of Malayali Cuisine

The cuisine of Kerala is linked in all its richness to the history, geography, demography and culture of the land. Since many of Kerala's Hindus are vegetarian by religion, and because Kerala has large minorities of Muslims and Christians that are predominantly non – vegetarians, Kerala cuisine has a multitude of both vegetarian and dishes prepared using fish, poultry and meat.

For over 2000 years, Kerala has been visited by ocean – goers, including traders from Greece, Rome, the eastern Mediterranean, Arab countries, and Europe (see History of Kerala). Thus, Kerala cuisine is a blend of indigenous dishes and foreign dishes adapted to Kerala tastes. Coconuts grow in abundance in Kerala, and consequently, grated coconut and coconut – milk are widely used in dishes and curries as a thickener and flavouring ingredient. In fact, the literal meaning of Kerala is Land of Coconuts Kerala's long coastline, numerous rivers and backwater networks, and strong fishing industry have contributed to many sea – and river – food based dishes.

Pre – independence Kerala was split into the princely states of Travancore and Kochi in the south, and the Malabar district in the north; the erstwhile split is reflected in the recipes and cooking style of each area. Both Travancore and Malabar cuisine consists of a variety of vegetarian dishes using many vegetables and fruits that are not commonly used in curries elsewhere in India including plantains, bitter gourd ('*paavaykka*'), taro ('*chena*'), Colocasia ('*chembu*'), Ash gourd ('*kumbalanga*'), etc.

However, their style of preparation and names of the dishes may vary. Malabar has an array of vegetarian and non – vegetarian dishes such as pathiri (a sort of rice – based pancake, at times paired with a meat curry), porotta (a layered flatbread, said to come from South – East Asia), and the Kerala variant of the popular biriyani, probably from Arab lands. Central Travancore region boasts of a parade of dishes that is largely identified with the Christians of the region.

In addition to historical diversity, the cultural influences, particularly the large percentages of Muslims and Syrian Christians have also contributed unique dishes and styles to Kerala cuisine, especially non – vegetarian dishes. The meat eating habit of the people has been historically limited by religious taboos. Brahmins eschew non vegetarian items. However, most of modern day Hindus do not observe any dietary taboos, except a few who belong to upper caste (Nambudiris, Nairs of Malabar). Muslims do not eat pork and other items forbidden by Islamic law.

Features of Kerala cuisine:

- **Kuttanad** is known as the —Rice Bowl of India‖, and thus the staple food of the Kerala, like most South – Indian states is *rice*. Unlike other states, however, many people in Kerala prefer *parboiled rice (Choru)* (rice made nutritious by boiling it with rice husk). A variety of *red rice called Carmague rice* is also very commonly used.
- Apart from rice, other sources of starch include **tapioca and wheat.**

- *Coconut (thenga)* is the chief ingredient here. Coconuts grow in abundance in Kerala, and consequently, coconut kernel, (sliced or grated) coconut cream and coconut milk (*thenga pal*) are widely used in dishes for thickening and flavoring. It is used fresh and dried. *Its oil is used as the cooking medium.* Palm oil and vegetable oil also finds limited use.
- Owing to the weather and the availability of spices, the Kerala cuisine is **richly spicy**specially the hot ones. The main spices used are cinnamon, cardamom, ginger, green and red peppers, cloves, garlic, cumin seeds, coriander, turmeric, and so on.
- Few fresh herbs are used which mainly consist of the commonly used **curry leaf**, and the occasional use of fresh coriander and mint.
- **Vegetarian dishes** often consist of fresh spices that are liquefied and crushed to make a paste – like texture to dampen rice.
- Kerala's long coastline, numerous rivers and backwater networks, and strong fishing industry have contributed to many sea and river food based dishes. Arabian influence is preparation of biryani and fish. The Malabar coast of Kochi, Trivandrum, and Kovalam have enough of fresh fish supplies. In Alleppy to the use of seafood is common.
- **Tamarind (puli) and lime** are used to make sauces sour in North Malabar areas; the Travancore region uses only *kodampuli* (Garcinia cambogia), as *sour sauces or gravies* are very popular in Kerala.
- Kerala cuisine also has a *variety of* **pickles and chutneys**, and *crunchy pappadums.*
- The back garden of almost every household provides *green chillies, plantains, papaya, jackfruit, pumpkin and other vegetables* and so these are very commonly used in the cuisine.
- Steaming, blanching, simmering are commonly used *cooking methods.* Fermentation is also used.
- **Jaggery or molasses**is a common sweetening ingredient, although white sugar is also used.
- **Kerala is known for its traditional banquet or *sadhya*,** a vegetarian meal served with boiled rice and a host of side – dishes served especially during special occasions and festivals.

Variation of Kerala cuisine: Based on the religions and topography, —Keraliya paachaka shailee‖ is sub divided into three distinct but very overlapping categories. The differences show up only in a few of the dishes which are a specialty that are made on religious occasions.

Hindu Cuisine: Being a Hindu state from the very beginning, almost everything that all the other cuisines have is similar or slightly modified version of the original Hindu cuisine in Kerala; all but with a few variations giving way to the vast diversity to Keralite cuisine. To understand it furthermore we shall discuss the other two cuisines.

Malabar or Mappila Cuisine: Malabar forming the northern Kerala is a mix of cultures. Malabar cuisine is noted for its variety of pancakes and steamed rice cakes made from pounded rice. This Arab – influenced cuisine of the Mappila community offers some of the most flavourful dishes in Kerala. The use of fragrant spices, especially pepper, cardamom and cloves, is the highlight. Malabar food is generally mildly flavoured and gently cooked. The mutton is cooked tender, the rice flaky and delicately spiced with the right portions of condiments, to leave the taste lingering for long. Special brand of Malabari Moppila biriyani. Biriyani – whether mutton, chicken, fish or prawn – is the USP of Malabar cuisine. Other outstanding dishes are *muttamaala* (egg garland), *kadukkanira chathu* (stuffed mussels) and *kozhinira chathu* (stuffed chicken).

Syrian Christian (Suriani): The cuisine of the state of Kerala, India, is influenced by its large Christian minority. A favourite dish of Kerala Syrian Christians is stew: chicken, potatoes and onions simmered gently in a creamy white sauce flavoured with black pepper, cinnamon, cloves, green chillies, lime juice, shallots and coconut milk. They also prepare stews with chicken, lamb, and duck. Places like Kottayam, a Christian centric zone has *arikada*, *appam*, *rice*, *banana fry*, and *payasam* served during marriage and other parties. Other dishes include *piralen* (chicken stir – fries), meat thoran (dry curry with shredded coconut), fiery, sardine and duck curries, and meen molee (spicy stewed fish). This is eaten with appam. Appams, *kallappams*, or *vellayappams* are rice flour pancakes which have soft, thick white spongy centres and crisp, lace – like edges. *Meen vevichathu* (fish in fiery red chilli sauce) is another favourite item. In addition to chicken and fish, Syrian Christians also eat red meat. For example, *erachi* or *larthiathu* is a beef or mutton dish cooked with spices.

Christian cookery specially caters to people with a sweet tooth – crunchy *kozhalappam*, *achappam*, *cheeda*, *churuttu* etc.

Traditional Keralite kitchen: In the traditional homes of Kerala called *tharavads*, the cooking centres around the hearth, that has four to six stoves called *adupus*. Chopping and food preparation is accomplished on the kitchen table, using little wood handled knives for vegetables and a large cleaver for meat and seafood. Equally important is the little stone mortar and pestle in which small amounts of spices or chillies are crushed or pounded. The kitchen countertop holds the grinding stone on which most of the daily spices are crushed or ground. It also contains several large blocks of wood on which meat and fish are chopped. A deep stone sink for pot wash can be found in a smaller room adjoining the kitchen.

A storeroom, adjacent to the kitchen is where large reserves of staples and farm produce are kept. Larger homes have separate rooms for various tasks. For e.g., the granary or *nellu ara* is a large wooden room within the kitchen where the food grains are stored, or the *ora pera*, which is a large room in which large amounts of rice flour, halwa, snacks and fruits called *palaharam* are prepared. Many traditional kitchens function in the above manner even today with a smaller modern kitchen close to the main kitchen, housing conveniences like gas stoves, electric grinders, microwave ovens and coffee makers.

A Typical Malayali day of Meals:

Breakfast:

Kerala cuisine offers many delicious vegetarian breakfast dishes that are often relatively unknown outside the state. These include Puttu (made of rice powder and grated coconut, steamed in a metal or bamboo holder) and kadala (a curry made of black chana), iddali (fluffy rice pancakes), sambar, dosa and chutney, pidiyan, Idiyappam (string hoppers – also known as Noolputtu and Nool – Appam), Paal – Appam, a circular, fluffy, crisp – edged pancake made of rice flour fermented with a small amount of toddy or wine, etc. Idiyapam and Paalappam are accompanied by mutton, chicken or vegetable stew or a curry of beef or fish moilee (the most common dish is fish in a coconut based sauce).Lunch and dinner

The staple food of Kerala is rice. Parboiled rice (Choru) (rice made nutritious by boiling it with rice husk) is more preferred. Kanji (rice congee), a kind of rice porridge, is also popular. Tapioca, called kappa in Kerala, is popular in central Kerala and in the highlands, and is frequently eaten with fish curry. Rice is usually consumed with one or more curries. Accompaniments with rice may include upper is (dry braised or sautéed vegetables), rasam, chips, and/or buttermilk (called moru). Vegetarian dinners usually consist of multiple courses, each involving rice, one main dish (usually sambar, rasam, puli – sherry), and one or more side – dishes.

Popular vegetarian dishes include sambar, aviyal, Kaalan, theeyal, thoran (dry curry), pulisherry (morozhichathu in Cochin and the Malabar region), olan, erisherry, pulinji, payaru (mung bean), kappa (tapioca), etc. Common non – vegetarian dishes include stew (using chicken, beef, lamb, or fish), traditional or chicken curry (Nadan Kozhi Curry), chicken fry (Kozhi Porichathu/Varuthathu), fish/chicken/mutton molly(fish or meat in light gravy), fish curry (Meen Curry), fish fry (Karimeen Porichathu/ Varuthathu), lobster fry (Konchu Varuthathu), Spicy Beef Fry (Beef Ularthiyathu), Spicy Steamed Fish (Meen Pollichathu) etc. Biriyani, a Mughal dish consists of rice cooked along with meat, onions, chillies and other spices. Although rice and tapioca may be considered the original Kerala starch staples, wheat, in the form of chappatis or parathas (known as porottas in Kerala), is now very commonly eaten, especially at dinner time. Grains such as ragi and millet, although common in the arid parts of South India, have not gained a foothold in Kerala.

Sweets and Desserts:

Due to limited influence of Central Asian food on Kerala, the use of sweets is not as widespread as in North India. Kerala does not have any indigenous cold desserts, but hot/warm desserts are popular. The most popular example is undoubtedly the payasam: a preparation of milk, coconut extract, sugar, cashews, dry grapes, etc. Payasam can be made with many base constituents, including Paal payasam (made from rice), Ada payasam (with Ada, a flat form of rice), Paripu payasam (made from dal), Pazham pradhamam (made from banana), Gothambu payasam (made from wheat). Ada payasam is especially popular during the festival of Onam. Most payasams can also be consumed chilled. Fruit, especially the small yellow bananas, are often eaten after a meal or at any time of the day. Plantains, uncooked or steamed, are popularly eaten for breakfast or tea.

Other popular sweets include Unniappam (a fried banana bread), pazham – pori (plantain slices covered with a fried crust made of sweetened flour), and kozhukkatta (rice dumplings stuffed with a sweet mixture of molasses, coconut etc.). Cakes, ice – creams, cookies and puddings are equally common. Generally, except for payasam, most sweets are not eaten as dessert but as a tea – time snack.

Pickles and other side – dishes: Kerala cuisine also has a variety of pickles and chutneys, and crunchy pappadums, banana chips, jackfruit chips, kozhalappam, achappam, cheeda, and churuttu.

Beverages:

Being mostly a hot and humid area, Keralites have developed a variety of drinks to cope with thirst. A variety of what might be called herbal teas is served during mealtimes. Cumin seeds, ginger or coriander seeds are boiled in water and served warm or at room temperature. In addition to the improved taste, the spices also have digestive and other medicinal properties. Sambharam, a diluted buttermilk often flavoured with ginger, lime leaves, green chilli peppers etc. was very commonly drunk, although it has been replaced to some extent by soda pop. Coffee and tea (both hot) drunk black, or with milk and white sugar or unrefined palm sugar (karippatti), are commonly drunk. Numerous small shops dotted around the land sell fresh lime juice (called naranga vellam, or bonji sarbat in Malayalam), and many now offer milk shakes and other fruit juices. The people of Kozhikode, which is mostly muslim dominated enjoy Mappila (biriyani) and Kawa, a traditional tea, similar to Kehwa of Kashmir.

Sadhya:

Sadhya is Traditional Big Feast. An improperly laid Ela (plantain Leaf) is an indicator. The food is served on a plantain leaf. The narrow tip of the leaf should face the left and service should start from the bottom half of the leaf, where a small yellow banana is placed followed by jaggery coated banana chips, plain banana chips and papadum. Then beginning from the top half of the leaf, lime curry, mango pickle, inji puli, lime pickle, thoran, Vegetable Stew or Olan, Avail (thick Mixture of Vegetables), Pachadi (Raw Mango and Curd Mixture), Elisseri (Vegetable like Pumpkin or Green Banana) and khichdi. Rice served at the bottom centre. Sambhar and kalan are then poured on rice. Once the meal is over, the pradaman dessert is served and after that rasam is taken with rice or even separately.

Onasadhya:

Onam heralds the harvest festival and is also according to folklore the time of the year when the king Mahabali, the legendary ruler of an ancient golden era in Kerala, returns from the depths of the nether world to visit his beloved subjects.

Onasadhya is the most delicious part of the grand festival called Onam. It is considered to be the most elaborate and grand meal prepared by any civilisation or cultures in the world. It's a feast which if enjoyed once is relished for years. Onasadhya is prepared on the last day of Onam, called Thiruonam. People of Kerala wish to depict that they are happy and prosperous to their dear King Mahabali whose spirit is said to visit Kerala at the time of Onam.

Rice is the essential ingredient of this Nine Course Strictly Vegetarian Meals. All together there are 11 essential dishes which have to be prepared for Onasadhya. Number of dishes may at times also go up to 13. Onasadhya is so elaborate a meal that it is called meals, even though it is consumed in one sitting. There are almost 64 dishes served. Onasadhya is consumed with hands; there is no concept of spoon or forks.

Traditional Onasadhya meal comprises of different varieties of curries, upperies – things fried in oil, pappadams which are round crisp flour paste cakes of peculiar make, uppilittathu – pickles of various kinds, chammanthi – the chutney, payasams and prathamans or puddings of various descriptions. Fruits and digestives are also part of the meal.

The food has to be served on a **tender Banana leaf**, laid with the end to the left. The meal is traditionally served on a mat laid on the floor. A strict order of serving the dishes one after the other is obeyed. Besides, there are clear directions as to what will be served in which part of the banana leaf.

Utensils of a traditional Malayali Kitchen:

- *Chembu:* It is a vessel made out of copper or brass used for steaming or boiling food. Now aluminium is more frequently used.
- *Cheena chetty:* Frying pan
- *Puttu kuti:* It is used for steaming rice flour paste called puttu. It has a round base pot in which water is boiled, and a tall cylindrical tube above this base in which rice flour and coconut are layered and steamed.
- *Cheena chatti:* Literally meaning —Chinese potǁ, this is a round – bottomed vessel with two handles similar to a wok. The round bottom

spreads the heat evenly through the base and into the food; which makes it ideal for sautéing and deep frying.

- *Appam chatti:* This is a heavy round bottomed vessel made of iron with a lid similar to the cheena chatti. It is used to prepared stews.
- *Kalam:* It is a large rice vessel in which water, tapioca or rice is boiled.
- *Urali:* This is a wide mouthed squat vessel made of bell metal which gradually warms up and retains heat for a long time. It is multipurpose: it is used to fry and roast meat, to cook halwas and to dry roast rice flour.
- *Meen chatti:* It is a round bottomed earthen pot used to prepare fish curries.
- *Cherava:* This is used to grate coconut. It has got ridged metal blades resting on a wooden platform. The coconut is first halved and then grated on this equipment.
- *Ural and ulakka:* A *ural* is a large drum – shaped stone used for pounding rice and spices with a long wooden rod called *ulakka.*
- *Ammi and ammikuuti:* This equipment contains a flat grinding stone called *ammi* with a cylindrical stone called *ammikuuti* and is used for grinding wet masalas.
- *Thavi:* These are ladles made from the coconut shells, which have a long bamboo handle. *Muttamala*, a speciality dessert, is made by passing egg yolks through a one – holed thavi into a sugar syrup.
- *Idooni achu:* This is a noodle press for preparing thin vermicelli from rice doughs. These vermicelli are used for *idiyappams and puttus.*
- *Kudukka:* Traditionally, earthenware clay pots are used for cooking food in Kerala.
- *Uruli:* Brass cooking pot.

Festival Specials of Malayali Dishes:

1. **Ada pradhaman**: It is a kheer made with ada rice, jaggery and coconut milk.
2. **Ada pradhaman**: Rice flakes, jaggery, coconut milk garnished with cashew nut.
3. **Appams**: It is a rice pancake with a soft and thick centre and a crispy, paper thin outside. Prepared in Appam moulds.

4. **Avial**: Local vegetables cooked in crushed grated coconut, shallots and cumin finished with yoghurt.

5. **Chatti pathiri**: It is layered sweet pastry, similar to Italian Lasagna. This sweet is made of flour, egg and oil and specially seasoned with cardamom and other spices along with nuts and dry fruits

6. **Cheera thoran**: Red spinach and grated coconut dry vegetable curry

7. **Chemeen pollichathu** (pan seared prawns): Prawns are marinated in spices and lime juice, and cooked in coconut milk.

8. **Erachi ishtu**: This is a meat stew from the Moplah cuisine. Meat cubes and potatoes are cooked with coconut milk, chillies and ginger garlic paste.

9. **Erachi puttu**: Steamed rice cake with coconut and minced meat.

10. **Erachi ularthiyathu**: Similar to Erachi varattiyathu, but can be prepared with coconut, fenugreek instead of aniseed and turmeric.

11. **Erachi varattiyathu** (beef masala): This is a dish consisting of beef cubes cooked in a thick gravy. The preparation is finished by adding garam masala, chopped coriander, chopped curry leaves and lemon juice.

12. **Erissery**: A sweet and spicy curry with the sweetness from the pumpkin and coconut. Erissery is one of the main side dish (kootan) served in sadhya.

13. **Idiyappam**: These are thin vermicelli of rice which can be eaten during any meal. To make this rice flour is cooked with hot water until it resembles a dough. It is then pressed through idooni achu or a vermicelli press.

14. **Idiyappam**: It is basically made of rice flour, water and salt. Numerous strands of vermicelli are entwined together to make this version of an appam. It is also known as noolappam.

15. **Ishtews**: stew where chunks of any kind of meat is smothered in a silky, rich, dreamy coconut curry

16. **Kadala curry**: Black chickpeas curry.

17. **Kai pola**: Soft banana cake with cardamom and nuts.

18. **Koon unakkamulagu ularthiyathu**: Semolina crumbed beetroot and banana Flower with ground spices

19. **Kozhi curry** (Malbari curry): The ingredients used in the preparation of this dish are coconut oil, cinnamon, cardamom, cloves, sliced onions, garlic, crushed shallots, and crushed green chillies, ginger and garlic along with masala powders. This is cooked in coconut milk and the tempering is done with curry leaves, mustard seeds, and coconut oil and

is poured over it.

20. **Kozhikaal**: These are fritter, like starters made of tapoica, especially served in the evenings.

21. **Kunjurotti**: Rice dumplings served with spicy curry of mutton, fish or chicken.

22. **Malabar parota**: It has a flaky, crispy and crumbly texture which melts in your mouth and leaves behind a sweet yet savoury taste.

23. **Malabari paratha**: These are flaky shallow – fried parathas often served with various veg and non – veg curries. The dough is kneaded to a very soft consistency and then flattened by flipping on the table. Oil is then applied on the thin dough and rolled like a lachcha paratha. It is shallow fried until crisp.

24. **Meen mappa** (fish curry): Pomfret fish spicy curry prepared along with coconut milk, onion, tomato, curry leaves and a melange of whole spices. This dish is best enjoyed with appams.

25. **Meen molee**: This is a fish preparation in a thin gravy in which different extracts of coconut milk is used along with sliced onions, slit green chillies, garlic and ginger. Ground masalas prepared with turmeric, a pinch of garlic, and red chillies are added and fried. Some tomatoes can also be added.

26. **Meen murringakka curry**: Sardines are cooked with pulp – y tamarind, coconut and drumsticks and then tempered with onions and red chillies.

27. **Meen porichathu** (shallow fried fish): This is a shallow fat fried fish preparation in which the fish is marinated with turmeric, lime juice and salt followed by a mixture of spices, ginger and garlic paste. It is served with roundels of onion, lemon wedges and fried curry leaves. The fishes commonly used for this preparation commonly include pomfret, kingfish and pearl spot cut into darne.

28. **Naadan kozhi curry**: The red piquant Kerala chicken curry is a perfect blend of spices and meat.

29. **Pachamoru**: This is a thirst quenching traditional drink from Kerala, also known by the names as Sambharam or Morum Vellam.

30. **Pal appam**: Pancakes made with fermented rice flour and toddy.

31. **Palada payasam**: A traditional dessert, prepared during the festival of Onam or any other occasion is a simple rice pudding or kheer, made in almost all the households across Kerala.

32. **Pathiri**: Thin rice pancakes served with meat or fish curry.

33. **Pazham nirachathu**: Robusta banana stuffed with coconut and jaggery, sautéed in ghee and sugar.

34. **Pazham pori**: Pazham Pori or Ethakka Appam is juicy banana fritters that are a favourite tea time snack in Kerala.Ripe bananas coated in plain flour and deep fried in oil.

35. **Puttu**: This is a breakfast item which is thin vermicelli strands of rice dough that are steamed in a special utensil called puttu kutti. Many kinds of puttus are made and these quite resemble the string hoppers made in Sri Lanka. In some places these are cylindrical steamed rice cake cooked with coconut shavings.

36. **Thalassery biryani**: Biryani made with kaima or biryani rice, indigenous spices, meat, and nuts.

37. **Thoran**: Dry vegetable dish usually made with chopped beans, cabbage, carrots etc. coconut is added to all.

38. **Unnakkaya**: Brinjal stuffed with egg, coconut and other ingredients and fried.

39. **Vattalappam**: Steamed custard with jaggery, egg and coconut milk.

Ocassions of Celebration:

Onam:

Onam (also known as Thiruvonam) is the state festival of Kerala. It is a 10 – day long festival, Onam is a well renowned Hindu festival observed by all its citizens, irrespective of caste, creed or community. It is a harvest festival celebrated once a year during the Malayalam month of Chingom (August – September) and also to mark the homecoming of great king Mahabali, who used to rule Kerala during the ancient period. Onam is traditionally celebrated with much joy and fervor. Some of the celebrations include creating a Pookalam (an extravagant arrangement of colourful flowers), visiting temples, feasting on an elaborate meal served on plantain leaves, gifting others with new clothes, participating in boat races held on the backwaters, a variety of sporting events and even Pulikkali (a tiger dance).

Thrissur Pooram Festival:

Thrissur Pooram is one of the famous temple festivals in Kerala and is celebrated in the Malayalam month of Medam (April – May). This festival is celebrated at the Vadakkunnathan Temple in Thrissur yearly and is celebrated for almost 36 hours with traditional puja, displays a spectacular procession of elephants and drummers and ending with extreme fireworks. The festival is celebrated to worship Lord Shiva and involves color, music, and religion.

Kerala Boat Festival:

Kerala is known around the world for its backwaters. The beautiful river, lakes and Arabian Sea are all the part of these backwater rides, where you can also visualize the boat festivals of Kerala. Boat Festival is enhanced with different sizes of the boats, where you can see the team spirit among participants, great enthusiasm among the riders and people cheering each other all around the place.

Theyyam Festival:

Theyyam is one of the most popular festivals celebrated in Kerala from December to April where more than 400 types of cultural dances, performed by peopled dressed as deities. The performer goes through three stages of learning: the first stage is of adorning themselves with colors, flowers, and mask; the second stage involves self – torture and the third stage is all about dancing on a rhythm. This festival is celebrated with huge fun which brings the new level of pleasure in the life of the attendees.

Vishu Festivals:

Vishu marks the beginning of Malayali year and is one of the most important and famous festivals of Kerala and which is an auspicious festival celebrated by Hindus on the first day of the Malayalum month of Medam (April – May). The most significant ritual observed during Vishu is the Kani Kanal (meaning _first sight'), as it is believed that the fortunes of the upcoming year depend on what object is seen first on the morning of Vishu. Mostly celebrated at home, a pooja with the family and the evening feast are the highlights of this Hindu festival.

Attukaal Pongala:

This festival is celebrated only by the women folk of Kerala. Women all over the city cook their offerings and bring it to the Attukal temple, which is located near Thiruvananthapuram city. Attukal Devi is said to be an incarnation of Goddess Parvati, wife of Lord Shiva. This is one festival, where people celebrate it without remembering their religion, caste or colour. The sweet dish called _Pongala' (payasam) is prepared by the women in the morning and is ready by noon for the offering along with banana. This dish is made from boiled rice, jaggery, and coconut.

Christmas:

Christmas in Kerala is celebrated unlike anywhere else in the world. The ever growing Christian population here, has adapted the Christmas celebrations, infusing it with the spirit and culture of Kerala itself. The birth of Jesus Christ is observed with traditional church services and elaborate nativity arrangements, sharing the love of Christ and the peace of the season with families and neighbours.

Easter:

Easter is celebrated worldwide to signify the resurrection of Jesus Christ. As the Christians in Kerala account for about 23% of the state's population, Easter is observed with the same fervour as in the west and is marked by four distinct periods.

Bharani:

This spectacular festival is celebrated in the month of Malayalam month of Kumbham (February – March) dedicated to Goddess Bhagavathy. The yearly event at the Sree Kurumba Bhagavathy Temple located at Kodungalloor and Chettikulangara Temple near Mavelikara in Alappuzha. People take ceremonial procession to the temple to the tune of music, the beating of drums and ornamental umbrellas and worship decorated effigies of chariots, horses and dieties .

Makaravilakku Festival:

Makaravilakku is an annual festival that is celebrated in Sabrimala temple on the occasion of Makar Sakranti on 14th January each year. The idol of Lord Ayyappa is worshiped in the famous Ayyappa Temple in Sabarimala. A procession of people, dressed up in sacred attire, carries ornaments of Ayappan that are called Thiruvabharanam. The journey advents two days prior to Makara Jyothi Day from Pandalam.

Aranmula Uthrattathi:

This festival is celebrated with a ritual boat race held during the Onam festival The Aranmula boat race is a century old boat race that's celebrated on the occasion of Aranmula Uthrattathi. The snake boats move in pairs with an excited crowd cheering on the banks of the river Pampa. As per the legends, the boat carrying offerings to the temple Aranmula Parthasarathy was attacked by enemies, and neighbouring people sent their snake boats to protect it. Which is now a snake boat race celebrated during the festival.

Adoor Gajamela:

It is an annual 10 day long celebration is held at the Parthasarathy Temple in Adoor dedicated to Lord Krishna. Gaja in Sanskrit means elephant and mela is fair. Nine elephants in their ceremonial attire are paraded, as hundreds of visitors throng the temple gates to witness the regal spectacle. The festivities include Ashtamirohini, the birthday anniversary of Lord Krishna, Parichamuttukali – a martial art, Velakali – a symbolic dance of ancient warfare, Mayooranritham – a form of peacock dance and a significant number of cultural programs as a highlight.

Thiruvathira:

This festival is mostly celebrated in the month of either December or January. This festival is in total dedication to Lord Shiva and Kamdeva (God of love). All the devotees in temple for the Lord's blessing.

Muharram:

Muharram is observed by Muslims to mourn the martyrdom of Imam Hussain (Prophet Mohammed's grandson) who died in the bloody massacre at Karbala in 680 AD. There is a period of fasting, and then glittery Taziyas (tombs made of bamboo and paper to replicate Hussain's tomb) are created and carried out into the city streets. Huge processions follow these taziyas and people are seen beating their chests mourning the slaying of Hussain. At the end of the procession, devotees end their fast and give away clothes, food and money to the poor and the downtrodden.

Classical Malayali Recipes:

Ginger Pachadi:

Ingredients-

- Fresh ginger- 50 gm
- Gr. Chillies- 15 gm
- Musdtard seeds- 5 gm
- Onion- 100 gm
- Crated coconut -100 gm
- Thick curd- 350 gm
- Curry leaves- a sprig
- Salt- tt
- Oil- 30 ml

Method-

- Grind the coconut to fine paste.
- Julienne the ginger and soak in water for ½ hour.
- Chop onion and green chilies.
- Cook together in little water, ginger, green chilies and chopped onion.
- Beat the curd well and add the chopped ingredients, salt and cook together for 2 minutes.
- Heat oil in a separate pan, add a chopped onion, mustard seeds and curry leaves.
- When seeds crackle, add to curd mixture, stir well and remove.

Note: always use thick curd and do not over cook the curd as it will curdle.

Malayali fish curry:

Ingredients-

- Rohu fish- 700 gm
- Red chilies- 30 gm
- Coriander seeds- 2 tsp
- Turmeric- pinch
- Red onion- 150 gm
- Garlic- 8 flakes.
- Ginger- ½ ‖
- Curry leaves- 2 sprig
- Cocum- 30 gm
- Salt- tt
- Coconut oil- 60 ml
- Fat- 30 gm

Method -

- Clean, wash and cut the fish into 1‖ slices (tracon).
- Broil red chilies and coriander, make powder and grind again with turmeric, garlic and onion to fine paste.
- Soak cocum in little warm water.
- Chop ginger.
- In a heavy bottomed frying pan take curry leaves and the cocum. Mix together the ground paste, fat and fish.

- Arrange on pan, pour enough water to cover the fish, bring to a boil and simmer on slow fire till the fish is cooked.
- Pour fresh coconut oil and remove from the fire.

Avial: (Kerala Style)

Ingredients-

- Potatoes - 25 gm
- Brinjal - 225 gm
- Fr. beans - 55 gm
- Raw banana - 115 gm
- Pumpkin - 100 gm
- Coconut - 115 gm
- Thick sour curd - 55 gm
- Coconut oil - 50 ml
- Cumin - ½tsp
- Green chilli - 5 nos.
- Turmeric - pinch
- Curry leaves - 1 sprig
- Salt - to taste

Method-

- Peel, wash and cut he vegetables into baton shape.
- Cool in sufficient water adding turmeric and curry leaves.
- Grate coconut and grind coarsely with green chilies and cumin. Mix well with curd.
- When the vegetables are cooked add curd, salt and the ground mixture.
- Bring to boil on slow fire. Add coconut oil, stir well and remove. Ser

Malabari Parantha:

Ingredients-

- Maida-200 gm

- Water -to knead
- Ghee-50 ml
- Dry flour- for dusting

Method -

- Knead the flour into soft and pliable dough with the water. Cover and let rest for 30 minutes.
- Make 8 round and smooth balls. Roll into a round of about ¼ cm/ 1/8 " thickness.
- Smear the surface of this round, with ghee. Fold in ½, smear the surface with ghee again, and make another fold from corner to corner. Roll thinly without tearing.
- Heat the griddle (tava), and place one parantha on to it.
- When the edges start lifting, slightly, smear some ghee over it letting it trickle under it.
- Brown on both sides and serve.

Aval Payasam:

Ingredients-

- Aval (Flattened/Beaten Rice) – 2 cups
- Milk – 3 cups
- Sugar – 6 tbsp (Adjust according to desired sweetness)
- Powdered Cardamom (Elakka) – 1 tsp
- Condensed Milk – 4 tbsp
- Ghee – 2 + 1 tbsp
- Cashews – 10 to 12
- Raisins – 8 to 10
- Salt – a pinch

Method-

- Wash the Beaten Rice thoroughly. Drain and keep aside.
- Heat 2 tbsp ghee in a non-stick pan and add the beaten rice. Lightly roast it for a few minutes until it becomes crisp.

- In a wide pan, heat 2 cups of milk. Add the roasted beaten rice, sugar and cardamom powder.
- Keep stirring so that the milk doesn't stick to the bottom of the pan. Add a pinch of salt to balance the taste.
- Cook the beaten rice for around ten minutes until it has softened.
- When the Beaten Rice is cooked, add 1 more cup of milk. Simmer the Payasam for a few more minutes stirring frequently.
- Reduce heat and add condensed milk. Keep stirring for another 2-3 minutes and then remove the Paysam from stove top.
- In a separate pan, heat 2 tbsp ghee. Throw in the cashews and raisins and fry until the cashews begin to brown. Add the fried cashews and raisins to the Payasam.
- Serve this yummy Aval Pyasam hot or cold.

Chicken Banana Wadas:

Ingredients -

- 4 No Raw Bananas,
- 100g Chicken mince, boil,
- 50g Semolina roasted (Rawa),
- 50g Green peas, boil, Oil to fry,
- 50g Onions, finely chopped,
- 2 tsp Ginger garlic paste,
- 1 Tbsp coconut, desiccated,
- 2 tsp Cumin powder,
- ½ sprig Coriander leaves, chopped,
- Salt to taste.

Method-

- Mix and mince the boiled bananas, chicken mince, roasted semolina (rawa) and green peas together,
- Heat two teaspoons of oil in a pan.
- Add the chopped onions and ginger garlic paste. Fry for three minutes.
- Add desiccated coconut and sauté for two minutes.

- Add the banana, chicken minced mixture along with salt, cumin powder and the finely chopped coriander leaves
- Mix well, stirring for a few minutes.
- When cool, knead the mixture to pliable dough.
- Divide the dough into lemon sized portions and roll into a small round patties.
- Heat oil into a *kadhai* and deep-fry the *wadas* till golden brown.
- Serve hot with tomato ketchup or mint chutney.

Banana Uthappa:

Ingredients -

- 4 No Raw Bananas,
- 4 No Potatoes,
- 50g Green peas, boil,
- 2 Tbsp Semolina (rawa),
- 1 No Onion, finely chopped,
- 1 tsp Ginger garlic paste,
- 2 Tbsp Coconut, grated,
- 1 tsp Cumin seed,
- roasted, ½ tsp Chilli powder,
- ¼ tsp Garam masala powder,
- ½ tsp Amchur (Dry mango powder),
- Salt to taste,
- Oil for frying.

Method -

- Boil bananas and potatoes till fully done.
- While still warm, peel and mash them together.
- Roast the *rawa* lightly.
- Add *rawa*, chopped onions, ginger garlic paste and grated coconut to the mashed mixture.
- Add all the seasoning ingredients, mix well and knead to a soft dough.
- Divide the dough into eight portions.
- Flatten each dough balls into a disc and press a few green peas on top.

- Heat a little oil on a non-stick pan and fry the *uthappa* till done on both sides.
- Serve hot garnished with onion rings.

CHAPTER SIX

Kannada Cuisine

"The cuisine of Karnataka as any other Indian cuisine, is influenced by both Hindu and Muslim traditions brought by the different rulers of this region. The culinary fare offered by Karnataka is quite varied with each region of the state having its own unique flavour. "

Many factors and influences have contributed to enrich this culinary heritage. Though there are many similarities between the food of Karnataka and its southern neighbours, the typical Mysore cuisine is well known for its own distinctive textural forms and flavour with the dishes complementing and balancing each other.

The famous 'Bisi-Bela Bath', 'Uppittu' and 'Holighe' are the delicious and popular food items from this region. 'Mysore masala dosa' is another favourite from Karnataka and so is the coconut chutney.

*"**The Karnataka meal is traditionally** served on a 'patravali (banana leaf) or 'muttuga' leaves stitched together especially during festive occasions or when entertaining visitors. The meal is divided into two parts. It begins with servings of pickle, sliced lemon, 'raita' (yoghurt), dry vegetables and a bowl of spiced dal. Rice is served with plain yellow dal or 'varan' (lentil), papads, fat puris made from whole-wheat flour and 'shreekhand (sweetened yoghurt with saffron). "*

An aromatic vegetable and nut 'pulao' forms the latter part of the meal. Often the hostess ceremonially serves fragrant homemade ghee as a signal for the guests to begin eating. It is also customary for the guests to sing a few stanzas from scriptures to bless the food and the host before beginning.

For everyday meals, Huli (a cousin of the sambhar of Tamils) begins the meal and then comes 'saaru'. The 'saaru' is followed by 'chitranna' and then the sweet dish is served.

As one goes north within the state, the food begins to resemble that of Maharashtra. The cuisine of coastal Karnataka has similarities with the food of Kerala. There is, in fact, a large amount of correspondence in the food of the four southern states of Karnataka, Andhra Pradesh, Tamil Nadu and Kerala. But there are subtle distinctions and recognizable differences in flavour.

Karnataka's culinary culture revolves round three staple items- rice, 'ragiand 'jowar'. However, the people in the northern districts have a preference for wheat and jowar rotis (unleavened bread made of millet) eaten with spiced vegetable preparations.

"In rural Karnataka, 'ragi is widely used with each meal. This staple grain is steam cooked and rolled into balls the size of cricket balls and served with hot chutney or 'huli. The Kodavas or Coorgis, who are culturally quite different from the rest of the state, have an equally distinct cuisine."

They are perhaps the only Hindus who serve non vegetarian food and alcoholic drinks for their marriage ceremonies and traditional festivities.

Most of the **Coorg curries** - noted for their flavour and taste-are coconut based, lightly spiced and moderately sour. The coastal cuisine of Karnataka is as delightful as that of Coorg.

The **non-vegetarian** meal in Karnataka consists of meat and fish. Fish and seafood are available in plenty and since the majority are fisher-folk, the cuisine is simple, yet flavoursome.

Cooking meat is a simple art in Karnataka, quite unlike that in north India or Hyderabad. Mangalore coast specializes in varieties of seafood, which are prepared in much the same way as in the rest of the coastal areas.

"A typical Karnataka meal has many delicacies like kosambari, a salad made of the broken halves of the soaked green moong dal (lentil) minus its skin, spiced with salt, green chilli and mustard seed (oggarane) and mixed with tiny scrapings of coconut, cucumber and carrot and dressed with a little lime juice."

Then there are the playas which are vegetables steamed or boiled to retain the original colour and flavour. Sometimes, huli is replaced with a milder kootu. Tamarind is taboo for kootu, which is spiced with lots of pepper, cumin seeds and ground coconut. Also, no Kannada meal is complete without saaru a clear pepper broth. Other delectable sweets that come out of the Kannada kitchen are the shavige payasa made of vermicelli and sugar, hesaru bele made with green gram dal, and baadami hallu, which is, crushed almonds mixed with milk, sugar and saffron.

Other popular Karnataka specialties are 'bisi bele huli anna', which is created out of rice, dal, tamarind, chilli powder, and cinnamon. 'Kesari bhath' (a halwa made of semolina, sugar, and saffron), chiroti and Mysore pak are among the favourite sweets in Karnataka.

But the piece de resistance is the obbattu or holige a flat thin, wafer-like chappati filled with a mixture of jaggery, coconut and sugar and fried gently on a skillet.

Potha Parban is a day given to feasting on homemade sweets, pancakes and puffed rice. Instead of the daily fare of rice and fish curry, the rice harvest is made festive with the addition of jaggery syrup, coconut candy and condiments, to create a variety of recipes for this day.

Classical Kannada Recipes:

Porial (Mixed Vegetables)

Ingredients:

- 12 No Green beans, cut into ½ inch pieces,
- 3 No Small carrots, cut into 4 inch rounds,
- 2 No Medium potatoes, peeled and cut into ¼ inch cubes,
- 1 No Green peas, thawed if using frozen,
- ½ inch Ginger minced finely,
- 3 cloves Garlic, ground into a paste with a pinch of cumin seeds,
- 6 No Curry leaves,
- 1 cup Finely chopped red onions,
- 3 No Green chillies, chopped finely,
- 1 Tbsp Black mustard seeds,
- 4 tsp. Asafoetida,

- 1 tsp. Urad dal (white gram beans),
- 1 tsp Chana dal (yellow split peas),
- 1 tsp. Turmeric,
- 3 Tbsp Unsweetened coconut flakes,
- 2 Tbsp Limejuice,
- 3 Tbsp Canola oil,
- Salt to taste,
- 1 Tbsp Cilantro leaves, chopped finely,
- 1 No Small hot green chilli, chopped finely.

Method:

- Soak potatoes and peas in hot water for 20 minutes.
- Drain and set aside. (Omit this for frozen peas.)
- In a kadai, heat oil over medium flame, add the mustard seeds and cook until they crackle, add the chana daal, urad daal, asafoetida, garlic, ginger, curry leaves and the green chillies, sauté until the urad daal is a light golden colour.
- Add the onions. Sauté until the onions are Translucent.
- Now add the beans, potatoes, peas and carrots and sauté for a few minutes.
- Add a cup of water and bring to a boil.
- Cook on simmer, partially covered until vegetables are tender (app. 10 min.)
- Remove lid and cook uncovered to evaporate any excess liquid in the pan.
- Add the coconut and sauté for a minute or two.
- Pour in the lime juice and mix well.
- Garnish with chopped cilantro leaves and chopped green chillies.

Cucumber Pachadi:

(Raita of Cucumber in a flavoured Yoghurt Sauce)
Ingredients:

- 2 cups Plain non-fat curd,
- 1 No Cucumber, shredded,
- 2 No Green chillies, seeded and chopped finely,
- 8 No Curry leaves,
- 2 tsp. Canola oil,
- 1 tsp. heeng (asafoetida),
- 1 tsp. Mustard seeds,
- 2 No Dry whole red chillies,
- 1 tsp. Urad dal(white gram beans),
- Salt to taste.

Method:

- Whisk the yoghurt in a bowl until smooth.
- Add the shredded cucumber and the green chillies into the yoghurt and mix well.
- In a small skillet, add the canola and heat over a medium flame.
- When oil is hot add the mustard seeds.
- When they begin to crackle add the heeng, urad daal, dry red chillies and curry leaves.
- Cook until the dal is golden brown in colour.
- Pour this tempered oil over the yoghurt and mix well.
- Serve chilled with most any Indian meal.

Summary

Andhra, Tamil and Keralian food has earned much fame across the globe, particularly for scrumptious dishes like Dosa, Vada, Idli, Uttapam and Sambar. The region offers a wide variety of vegetarian and non – vegetarian dishes with each state holding its own uniqueness and food habits. Some authentic and popular dishes of these regions that are sure to delight taste buds include Chakra Pongal, Sambar and Vadai from Tamil Nadu; Rava Idli from Karnataka; Kadala Curry and Appam from Kerala; and Kebabs and Biryanis from Andhra Pradesh. These regions of India are known for their varied range of spices, many of which are being exported to different nations for centuries, like cinnamon, cardamom, nutmeg, cloves and pepper. The region is famous for a wide range of spicy foods with each state differing others predominantly from the spiciness of food, its different varieties and method of cooking. The staple food of locals of the region including some Brahmin communities is rice which is best savoured with Sambhar or curry. Tampering of different dishes remains almost the same with primary ingredients being mustard seeds, red chillies, curry leaves and oil among others. Availability of different root tubers, coconut and huge variety of fish has witnessed use of such items in various regional dishes. Ingredients like chana dal, urad dal, plantain, tamarind, ginger, garlic, coconut and snake gourd along with fresh green chillies and dried red chillies are used extensively in these cuisines.

Many of the exquisite and delectable cuisines of Andhra Pradesh indicate a profound influence of culinary styles of the Mughals on the cuisines of this place. The mouth – watering Andhra delicacies like Biryani, Kebabs and Kurmas among others that are usually heavy, spicy and hot in nature are sure to satiate the gastronomic enthusiasts. The traditional cuisines of Andhra are considered the spiciest among all other Indian cuisines and witness liberal use of tamarind and chilli powder that give the dishes a distinct tangy and hot flavour. Diverse ranges of cuisines are available in Andhra that differ mostly based on different regions. While the food of Rayalaseema district is quite similar to that of Tamil Nadu and eastern Karnataka due to its close proximity with these regions, the staple diet of the Telangana region, which has evolved into a new state, is rotis made of jowar and bajra. The Andhra costal region offers varied cuisines with unique flavour, courtesy the more fertile lands of the belt and also due to availability of variety of seafood. Some of the toothsome and finger – licking dishes include: Hyderabadi Biryani is made of Basmati rice, meat and selective rich spices. Other varieties of biryanis include Kachay Gosht ki Biryani and Dum ki Biryani. Achaari Subzi: a gravy preparation of vegetables having flavour of pickles. Dum ka Murgh: a chicken preparation made in Hyderabadi Style. Mirchi ka Salan: a chili and peanut curry that often accompanies the biryani. Baghara Baingan: a brinjal curry that often forms a side dish with the Hyderabadi Biryani.

The staple food of Tamil Nadu is rice which forms part of a typical Tamil meal and savoured with different mildly or richly spiced vegetarian and non – vegetarian dishes. Although most of the Tamilians barring the Brahmins and certain non – Brahmin communities are non – vegetarians, they usually consume vegetarian meals with meat intake being quite infrequent compared to other non – vegetarians across the globe. Traditionally, several dishes are served during the main meal that is typically savoured with rice as staple. These include: Sambar or sambhar, a very popular South Indian stew that is prepared with lentils, vegetables and tamarind. Rasam, a tamarind – based soupy dish prepared with tomato, cumin, pepper, chilli pepper and can also comprise of any combination of vegetables with lentils. Kuzhambu, a gravy dish made of toor dal, urad dal, tamarind and other spices that can include different vegetables. Thayir that is curd which when taken with rice is called 'Thayir Sadam' where Sadam means rice.

Among the different regions of Tamil Nadu, cuisines of Chettinad, a region that falls in the Sivaganga district situated in southern part of the state, has earned huge fame for its spicy and aromatic dishes, particularly the non – vegetarian ones. The meaning of Chettinad itself is a social caste that is skilled in preparing food and the Chettinads are regarded as great chefs. The unique hot and pungent flavour of the dishes seasoned with grounded spices, the boiled egg toppings on the meals, the salted vegetables and sun – dried meat are some of the distinct features of this cuisine. Some of the popular vegetarian dishes of the area include dosa, sambar, rasam, thayir sadam, paniyaram, kozhakattai and adikoozh. Different non – vegetarian dishes are made of chicken, mutton, crab, fish, prawn and lobster, some of the selected ones are fish fry, Chettinad pepper chicken and Karuvattu Kuzhambu.

Kerala cuisine is varied, but best categorized according to the different local communities. The more famous ones are the Malabari Muslim dishes and the Syrian Christian dishes. Availability of coconut which is also the prime export item of the state has made it a fundamental component of Kerala cooking whether used as an ingredient or in oil form extracted from the nut. Availability of seafood in the coastal belt of the state makes it almost a daily consume. The common breakfast items include dosai, idli, porotta with mutton or chicken curry, vegetable stew, duck roast and chicken or mutton stew among various other dishes. Different vegetarian dishes include aviyal, sambar, rasam, kichadi, pachady and olan to mention a few. There is a wide variety of non – vegetarian dishes with some of the popular ones being Malabari Fish Curry, Pork Mappas, Malabar Biriyani, Meen Thoran – a fish preparation with coconut, Duck Curry, Pork Vindallu, Shrimp Coconut Curry, Fish Fry and Fish Curry. The various snacks items are banana fry, cutlets, cakes, halwas and payasam among others.

The cuisine of Karnataka as any other Indian cuisine, is influenced by both Hindu and Muslim traditions brought by the different rulers of this region. The culinary fare offered by Karnataka is quite varied with each region of the state having its own unique flavour. Many factors and influences have contributed to enrich this culinary heritage. Though there are many similarities between the food of Karnataka and its southern neighbours, the typical Mysore cuisine is well known for its own distinctive textural forms and flavour with the dishes complementing and balancing each other.

CHAPTER EIGHT

Glossary of South Indian Cuisine

1. **Aadi Perukku:** Monsoon festival of Tamil Nadu.
2. **Adai:** Adai is a healthy, protein rich & nutrient dense Breakfast made of mixed lentils & spices. It is one of the most commonly eaten foods from Tamil cuisine.
3. **Addaikal:** Thick griddle plate usually used to cook addai
4. **Adupus:** Malyali name for cooking stove
5. **Akakara:** Telugu name for spine gourds, used for making sambhars.
6. **Ammas:** Village Goddess of Andhra Pradesh.
7. **Ammikuuti:** Wet masala grinder (in Malyalam)
8. **Avapettina kura:** Mustard seed (In Telugu)
9. **Badam – ki – Jhab:** Marzipan in Malalayayli cuisine.
10. **Bharani:** Malayali festival dedicated to Goddess Bhagavathy.
11. **Billavakka:** Andhra snacks prepared with rice flour and deep fried
12. **Bommidala Pulusu:** Malayali fish stew
13. **Booralu:** Malayali name for laddoo
14. **Boti Jhammi:** Nizami kebab made with meat and intestines of goat.
15. **Cheena chatti:** Chinese wok in Malayali
16. **Chembu:** Malayali name for calocasia.
17. **Cherava:** Malayali utensil used to grate coconut.
18. **Chippa:** Clay pot iused to cook meat in Nizami cuisine.
19. **Choru:** Parboiled rice (in Malayali)
20. **Dalcha:** Also known as kaddu ka dalcha, is an Indian lentil – based curry originating from Hyderabad. Primary ingredients are mutton, chana dal

and tamarind.

21. **Dosa Thiruppi**: Flat slicer used to lift dosa (in Tamil)

22. **Dum Ke Baingan**: Charcoal roasted brinjal, cooked in spices (Nizami cuisine)

23. **Eyya Chombu**: It is made of pure tin. The best vessel to make Rasam traditionally in Tamil cuisine.

24. **Garijelu**: Deep fried dumpling with a sweet coconut and sugar filling inside. (Nizami cuisine)

25. **Gongura**: Widely eatem leafy plant form Andhra Pradesh.

26. **Haleem**: It is a type of stew popular Hyderabadi cuisine. It includes wheat or barley, meat and lentils.

27. **Jaadilu**: Telegu name of traditional pickle jars used to store home – made pickles.

28. **Jahaji Korma**: A spiced meat delicacy from Hyderabad, which has shelf – life of 40 – 45 days, suitable for long journeys.

29. **Kachchi biriyani**: In this all the biriyani materials are cooked together to refinements.

30. **Kalam**: An iron vessel in which rice or tapioca is boiled. (Malayali name)

31. **Katti**: Vegetable knife in Telegu.

32. **Kosta**: The Coastal Andhra region is around Krishna and Godavari delta regions

33. **Kozhinira chathu**: Stuffed chicken (Mapilla cuisine – Kerala)

34. **Lagan – ke – Kababs**: Kebabs cooked in lagan (big thali), cut into burfi shape.

35. **Lukmi**: Minced meat patty. A typical mince savoury or starter of the cuisine of Hyderabad.

36. **Menthipettina kura**: Fenugreek seed paste (Nizami cuisine)

37. **Nahari**: Thick mutton stew.

38. **Nizams**: The Royals of Hyderabad state.

39. **Ooragaya**: Its other name of Hyderabadi chutney.

40. **Pakki biriyani**: All the biriyani ingredients are cooked separately and then arranged and served.

41. **Palaharam**: Raw fruit diet during fasting (Tamil and Malayali)

42. **Pappu**: Telegu name for dal or lentil.

43. **Pongal**: It is a four – day – long harvest festival celebrated in Tamil Nadu. It is name of a dish also.

44. **Pushkaram**: Festival of Holi dip in Godavari, Krishna and Pennar in Andhra Pradesh.

45. **Puthandu:** Tamil New year.
46. **ubani – ka – Meetha:** Hyderabadi sweet made from apricots.
47. **Rayalaseema:** It is region in Andhra Pradesh on the other side of Krishna river.
48. **Sadhya:** Keralian banquet.
49. **Sakinalu:** A traditional snack from Hyderabad usually prepared during Sankranti festival made of rice flour and sesame seeds.
50. **Saral Vizha:** It is a novel festival celebrated in the month of August to commemorate waterfalls in the region of Kuttalam in Tamil Nadu.
51. **Sheer Korma:** Vermicelli kheer from Hyderabad.
52. **Thaipusam:** A Tamil festival in honour of Lord Murugan .
53. **Tharavads:** Traditional homes of Kerala.
54. **Thiruvathira:** A Keralian Hindu festival paying homage to lord Shiva.
55. **Thuruvammai:** Equipment used as coconut scrapper, peeling and cutting vegetables and cutting of fish and meat. (Tamil)
56. **Ugadi:** Telegu New year.
57. **Ulava charu:** Famous Hyderabadi soup made from Horsegram.
58. **Ulli akku kura:** Spring onion curry from Andhra Pradesh.
59. **Uruli:** Heavy metallic pot used to cook sambhar. (Tamil)

The Author

Dr. Anshumali Pandey, is a renowned & reliable name in the field of Education, Hospitality, Tourism and Tribal Food. He is a Teacher and Chef by profession, and also an Author, a Business Auditor, and an avid culinary traveller to the Indian Sub continental hinterlands. Dr. Anshumali Pandey is a Hospitality Educator (PhD) who specialises in Higher Education, Office Administration, Pay roll, HR, Labour Laws, Audit, and Procurement & Tender Process. He is an Author with 56 Publications consisting of 41 Books.

The books written by **Dr Anshumali Pandey** are essentially a banquet arising from an experience of over 25 years of Professional life and have boiled down to crisp and accurate writing on his favourite subjects. Hospitality Sector champion requires to be a specialist in many fields and Dr Pandey is one of them. His knowledge is evident from the spectrum of subjects which he has chosen for his books so far, which ranges from being a specialist chef, to Master of Human resources, to Education and to love for children, and topped with Spirituality.

Books written by the Author are –

1. Theory of Indian Cookery
2. Beauty and Irony of Silvassa Tourism
3. A Short Indian Food Story
4. Be Your Own Guide to Indian Cuisine
5. Cookery Fundamentals
6. History of Indian Food (2 Editions Printed)
7. The Great Indian Story Book for Children
8. Personal Budget: Easy Work Book
9. Online Classes Log Book
10. Dictionary Making Work Book for School Children
11. The Lazy Bed
12. Hindu Dharm (हिन्दू धर्म) (In Hindi Language)
13. Where is my coffee?
14. Your First Job is Never your Last (Volume 1)
15. You are Almost There (Quick Fix Resume and Interview Hacks)
16. Working for the Enemy? - A lesson in Career Management
17. Public Speaking for the Young

18. A Date With Coffee
19. How to be The Best Hotel Front Office Employee
20. Diploma in Food Production, The complete Syllabus
21. Diploma in F&B Service, The Complete Syllabus
22. Diploma in Front Office, The Complete Syllabus
23. The Time to Speak is Now
24. Munshi Premchand (Short Stories in English)
25. The Housekeeping Department, Text Book
26. Hitchhiker's Guide to Trekking in Uttarakhand
27. Uttarakhand, A divine Land for a Reason
28. Bachhon ke liye rochak kahaniyan (बच्चों के लिए रोचक कहानियाँ) (In Hindi Language)
29. Basic Communication Skills of English
30. The Basic Office Organisation Book for Start-ups
31. Hospitality HRM
32. Hospitality Marketing
33. Bakery Ingredients and Tools
34. Human Resource Management for Indian Professionals
35. The process of LAWFULLY operating a Hospitality business in India
36. Indian Classical Sweets: History, Tradition and Recipes
37. History of India's Himalayan Cuisine: Classical Cookery of Kashmir, Laddakh, Jammu, Himachal, Lahaul, Spiti, Garhwal, Kumaon.
38. Vindu: Andhra Cuisine (Part 1 of South Indian Trilogy)
39. Saappadu: Tamil Cuisine (Part 2 of South Indian Trilogy)
40. Sadya: Malayali Cuisine (Part 3 of South Indian Trilogy)
41. **South Indian Cuisine - The Researcher's Guide Book**

Connect with me: anshumali.pandey@gmail.com
https://notionpress.com/author/337004

Kindly scan this QR code for updates and pictures of the Author and his works.